KitchenAid®

Great
Baking
and More

D1123850

Publications International Ltd.

Favorite Brand Name Recipes at www.fbnr.com

© 2005 Publications International, Ltd.

Favorite Brand Name is a trademark of Publications International, Ltd.

Front cover photography and photography on pages 9, 17, 19, 21, 23, 25, 33, 37, 41, 43, 45, 47, 49, 51, 55, 61, 63, 65, 67, 69, 71, 73, 79, 83, 85, 95, 79, 107, 109, 111, 113, 115, 129, 133, 135, 137, and 139 by Stephen Hamilton Photographics, Inc.
Photographers: Tate Hunt, Jennifer Marx, Brian Wetzstein, Eric Coughlin
Photographer's Assistant: Annie Grimes, Raymond Barrera
Prop Stylists: Thomas G. Hamilton
Food Stylists: Kim Hartmann, Carol Smoler, Mary Helen Steindler, David Kennedy
Assistant Food Stylist: Thomas Sherman, Lillian Sakamaki

Pictured on the front cover: Double-Decker Butterscotch Brownies *(page 114).*
Pictured on the back cover (clockwise from top): Cappuccino Fudge Cupcakes *(page 80)* and Basic Egg Noodle Pasta *(page 72).*

ISBN-13: 978-1-4127-2320-6
ISBN-10: 1-4127-2320-5

Manufactured in China.

8 7 6 5 4 3 2 1

Nutritional Analysis: Nutritional information is given for the recipes in this publication. Each analysis is based on the food items in the ingredient list, except ingredients labeled as "optional" or "for garnish." When more than one ingredient choice is listed, the first ingredient is used for analysis. If a range for the amount of an ingredient is given, the nutritional analysis is based on the lowest amount. Foods offered as "serve with" suggestions are not included in the analysis unless otherwise stated.

Contents

KitchenAid® Stand Mixers **4**

Starters and Sides **8**

Essential Breads **32**

Extraordinary Entreés **56**

Classic Cakes **78**

Sweet Bites **102**

Delicious Desserts **128**

Glossary of Cooking Terms ... **152**

Recipe Index **157**

KitchenAid®

STAND MIXERS

Great cooking made

easy

We're pleased to bring you this book, *KitchenAid Great Baking & More*, a collection of incredible recipes written especially for the KitchenAid stand mixer and its attachments and accessories. We've included classic baking recipes that take full advantage of the power and versatility of your mixer, as well as great new ideas with fresh, exciting flavors.

When we chose the title, *Great Baking & More*, we did so deliberately. You'll find all the great baking recipes you've come to associate with KitchenAid, but you'll also find recipes for stunning appetizers, amazing entrées, and delectable side dishes. We're especially proud of the recipes that use the stand mixer in ways you might not expect, but we trust you'll be as pleased with all the recipes as we are.

The KitchenAid name has always stood for versatility, reliability, and durability. We first developed and marketed our classic stand mixer to home cooks in the early 1900s.

From the start, KitchenAid stand mixers were revolutionary appliances. For the first time, home cooks could use an electric mixer with beaters that moved in a "planetary action": As the beater rotates clockwise, it travels counter-clockwise around the bowl; this draws ingredients around the edge of the bowl into the center more efficiently and mixes all ingredients together more thoroughly than most other electric mixers.

In fact, KitchenAid stand mixers are so efficient you may need to adjust the mixing time called for in recipes you get from other sources. Mixing cake batters with a KitchenAid stand mixer, for example, generally will take half the time called for in most standard recipes.

And thanks to that same planetary action, when you do add ingredients, they can be placed as close to the edge of the bowl as possible, not directly onto the moving beater. This virtually guarantees that less material is thrown out of the bowl, meaning less mess and less cleanup for you! In fact, solid ingredients—chocolate chips, nuts, raisins, and so forth—generally need be folded in only during the last few seconds of mixing. That way they are less likely to sink to the bottom of the pan during baking.

SPEED CONTROL GUIDE

KitchenAid stand mixers can be set to any of 10 speeds to mix at exactly the speed best suited to your recipes. The most important speeds and their general uses are:

Speed	Use	General Uses
Stir	STIR	For slow stirring, combining, mashing, starting all mixing procedures. Use to add flour and dry ingredients to batter, add liquids to dry ingredients, and combine heavy mixtures.
Speed 2	SLOW MIXING	For slow mixing, mashing, faster stirring. Use to mix heavy batters and candies, start mashing potatoes or other vegetables, cut shortening into flour, mix thin or splashy batters, and mix and knead yeast dough. Use with Can Opener attachment.
Speed 4	MIXING, BEATING	For mixing semi-heavy batters, such as cookies. Use to combine sugar and shortening and to add sugar to egg whites for meringues. Medium speed for cake mixes. Use with: Food Grinder, Rotor Slicer/Shredder, and Fruit/Vegetable Strainer attachments.
Speed 6	BEATING, CREAMING	For medium-fast beating (creaming) or whipping. Use to finish mixing cake, doughnut, and other batters. High speed for cake mixes. Use with Citrus Juicer attachment.
Speed 8	FAST BEATING WHIPPING	For whipping cream, egg whites, and boiled frostings.
Speed 10	FAST WHIPPING	For whipping small amounts of cream or egg whites. Use with Pasta Maker and Grain Mill attachments.

NOTE: Will not maintain fast speeds under heavy loads, such as when using Pasta Maker or Grain Mill attachments.

NOTE: The Speed Control Lever can be set between the speeds listed in the above chart to obtain speeds 3, 5, 7, and 9 if a finer adjustment is required. Do not exceed Speed 2 when preparing yeast doughs as this may cause damage to the mixer.

BEATER STYLES

KitchenAid stand mixers come packaged with 3 types of beaters to provide exactly the style of mixing best suited to your recipes. These beaters and their uses are:

Beater Style	Use	Example Recipes
Flat Beater	mixing normal to heavy mixtures	biscuits, cakes, candies, cookies, creamed frostings, mashed potatoes, meat loaves, pie pastries, quick breads
Wire Whip	incorporating air into mixtures	angel food cakes, boiled frostings, eggs, egg whites, heavy cream, mayonnaise, some candies, sponge cakes
Dough Hook	mixing and kneading yeast doughs	breads, buns, coffee cakes, rolls

WHIPPING EGG WHITES

Place room temperature egg whites in clean, dry bowl. Attach bowl and wire whip to mixer. To avoid splashing, gradually turn to designated speed and whip to desired stage (see following chart:)

Number of Egg Whites	Speed
1	gradually increase to Speed 10
2 or more	gradually increase to Speed 8

MAKING WHIPPED CREAM

For best results, chill bowl and wire whip in refrigerator or freezer for 5 to 10 minutes before beginning. Pour cold whipping cream into chilled bowl. Attach bowl and wire whip to mixer. To avoid splashing, gradually turn to designated speed and whip to desired stage (see following chart):

Amount of Cream	Speed
½ cup or less	gradually increase to Speed 10
½ cup to 1 pint	gradually increase to Speed 8

NOTE: If more than 1 pint of whipped cream is desired, whip it in batches 1 pint at a time.

Starters
AND SIDES

Elegant openers

perfect for entertaining guests, and

side dishes with that little something

extra to round out any meal.

APPETIZER CREAM PUFFS WITH
CREAMY FETA OLIVE FILLING

(page 10)

APPETIZER CREAM PUFFS

Pictured on page 9   **YIELD:** 36 CREAM PUFFS

1 **cup water**	1 **cup all-purpose flour**
½ **cup (1 stick) butter or margarine**	4 **eggs**
¼ **teaspoon salt**	**Creamy Feta Olive Filling (recipe follows)**

Heat water, butter, and salt in a medium saucepan over high heat to a full rolling boil. Reduce heat and quickly stir in flour, mixing vigorously until mixture leaves sides of pan in a ball.

Place mixture in mixer bowl. Attach bowl and flat beater to mixer. Turn to Speed 2 and add eggs, one at a time, beating about 30 seconds after each addition. Stop and scrape bowl. Turn to Speed 4 and beat 15 seconds.

Drop dough onto greased baking sheets in 36 mounds placed 2 inches apart. Bake at 400°F for 10 minutes. Reduce heat to 350°F and bake 25 minutes longer. Turn off oven. Remove baking sheets from oven. Cut a small slit in side of each puff. Return pans to oven for 10 minutes, leaving oven door ajar. Cool completely on wire racks.

Cut puffs in half and pipe or spoon about 1 tablespoon **Creamy Feta Olive Filling** into each puff. Serve immediately.

CREAMY FETA OLIVE FILLING

YIELD: 2 CUPS

1 **package (8 ounces) light cream cheese**	⅓ **cup finely chopped kalamata or ripe olives**
4 **ounces tomato and basil-flavored feta, crumbled**	½ **teaspoon lemon pepper seasoning**
½ **cup light sour cream**	

Combine all ingredients in mixer bowl. Attach bowl and flat beater to mixer. Turn to Speed 2 and mix about 30 seconds, or until blended.

PER SERVING: (1 CREAM PUFF) ABOUT 72 CAL, 2 g PRO, 4 g CARB, 5 g FAT, 37 mg CHOL, 132 mg SOD.

SARDINE AND EGG FILLING
YIELD: 2 CUPS

1	**can (3½ ounces) skinless, boneless sardines, drained**
6	**hard-cooked eggs**
½	**small onion**
¼	**cup mayonnaise**
	Salt and pepper

Assemble Food Grinder using coarse grinding plate and attach to mixer. Turn to Speed 4 and grind sardines, eggs, and onion into mixer bowl.

Add mayonnaise, salt, and pepper. Attach bowl and flat beater to mixer. Turn to Speed 2 and mix 1 minute. Chill mixture thoroughly. Fill cream puffs just before serving as directed above for Creamy Olive Feta Filling.

PER SERVING: ABOUT 71 CAL, 3 g PRO, 3 g CARB, 5 g FAT, 70 mg CHOL, 70 mg SOD.

CRAB DILL FILLING
YIELD: 2 CUPS

2	**cans (6½ ounces each) crab meat, drained**
2	**stalks celery, cut into 1-inch pieces**
½	**small onion**
1	**tablespoon lemon juice**
¼	**teaspoon dill weed**
½	**cup mayonnaise**
	Salt and pepper

Assemble Food Grinder using coarse grinding plate and attach to mixer. Turn to Speed 4 and grind crab, celery, and onion into mixer bowl.

Add lemon juice, dill weed, mayonnaise, salt, and pepper. Attach bowl and flat beater to mixer. Turn to Speed 2 and mix 1 minute. Chill mixture thoroughly. Fill cream puffs just before serving as directed above for Creamy Olive Feta Filling.

PER SERVING: ABOUT 74 CAL, 3 g PRO, 3 g CARB, 6 g FAT, 41 mg CHOL, 134 mg SOD.

CHICKEN AND PINEAPPLE FILLING
YIELD: 2 CUPS

2	**cups cubed, cooked chicken**
2	**stalks celery, cut into 1-inch pieces**
1	**can (8 ounces) crushed pineapple, drained**
¼	**cup slivered almonds**
½	**cup mayonnaise**
¼	**teaspoon paprika**
	Salt and pepper

Assemble Food Grinder using coarse grinding plate and attach to mixer. Turn to Speed 4 and grind chicken and celery into mixer bowl.

Add pineapple, almonds, mayonnaise, paprika, salt, and pepper. Attach bowl and flat beater to mixer. Turn to Speed 2 and mix 1 minute. Chill mixture thoroughly. Fill cream puffs just before serving as directed above for Creamy Olive Feta Filling.

PER SERVING: ABOUT 87 CAL, 4 g PRO, 4 g CARB, 6 g FAT, 37 mg CHOL, 66 mg SOD.

SWEET POTATO PUFF

YIELD: 6 SERVINGS (½ CUP PER SERVING)

2	medium sweet potatoes, cooked and peeled	**2**	tablespoons butter or margarine
½	cup low-fat milk	**½**	teaspoon nutmeg
⅓	cup sugar	**½**	teaspoon cinnamon
2	eggs		Crunch Praline Topping (recipe follows)

Place potatoes in mixer bowl. Attach bowl and flat beater to mixer. Turn to Speed 2 and mix for about 30 seconds. Add milk, sugar, eggs, butter, nutmeg, and cinnamon. Turn to Speed 4 and beat for 1 minute. Spread mixture in greased 9-inch pie plate. Bake at 400°F for 20 minutes or until set. Clean bowl and beater. Prepare **Crunchy Praline Topping** while puff bakes.

Spread **Crunchy Praline Topping** on hot puff. Bake 10 minutes longer.

CRUNCHY PRALINE TOPPING

2	tablespoons butter or margarine, melted	**½**	cup chopped walnuts or pecans
¾	cup cornflake cereal	**¼**	cup firmly packed brown sugar

Place all ingredients in mixer bowl. Attach bowl and flat beater to mixer. Turn to Stir Speed and mix about 15 seconds.

PER SERVING: (½ **CUP) ABOUT 268 CAL, 6 g PRO, 35 g CARB, 12 g FAT, 2 mg CHOL, 176 mg SOD.**

TIROPETAS

½ **pound feta cheese, drained and crumbled**

1 **package (3 ounces) cream cheese**

½ **cup cottage cheese**

¼ **cup grated Romano cheese**

⅛ **teaspoon pepper**

Dash nutmeg

2 **eggs**

1 **pound frozen prepared phyllo dough, thawed**

1 **cup (2 sticks) butter or margarine, melted**

Place feta cheese, cream cheese, and cottage cheese in bowl. Attach bowl and flat beater to mixer. Turn to Speed 4 and beat until fluffy, about 1 minute. Stop and scrape bowl. Add Romano cheese, pepper, and nutmeg. Turn to Speed 2 and beat 30 seconds. Stop and scrape bowl. Turn to Speed 2 and add eggs, one at a time, beating 30 seconds after each addition. Increase to Speed 4 and beat 15 seconds.

Place 1 sheet phyllo dough on a flat surface. Cover remaining phyllo dough with a slightly damp towel. Brush sheet with butter, top with another sheet and brush again with butter. Cut lengthwise into strips, about 2½ inches wide. Place 1 teaspoon cheese mixture on a bottom corner of strip. Fold over into a triangle shape and continue folding like a flag. Brush with butter and place on greased baking sheet. Repeat with remaining phyllo dough and cheese mixture. Work quickly as phyllo dough dries out quickly. Bake at 350°F until golden brown, about 15 to 20 minutes. Serve immediately.

PER SERVING: **(3 APPETIZERS) ABOUT 268 CAL, 7 g PRO, 16 g CARB, 20 g FAT, 80 mg CHOL, 484 mg SOD.**

FIESTA CHEESECAKE APPETIZER

YIELD: 20 SERVINGS

2 packages (8 ounces each) light cream cheese, softened

1 package (1¼ ounces) taco seasoning mix

3 eggs

2 cups shredded Marble Jack cheese

1 can (4 ounces) green chilies

1 cup light sour cream

1 cup prepared salsa

Place cream cheese and taco seasoning mix in mixer bowl. Attach bowl and flat beater to mixer. Turn to Speed 6 and beat about 1½ minutes, or until fluffy. Stop and scrape bowl. Turn to Speed 4 and add eggs, one at a time, beating about 15 seconds after each addition. Stop and scrape bowl. Add cheese and green chilies. Turn to Stir Speed and mix 15 seconds.

Pour mixture into greased 9-inch springform pan. Bake at 350°F for 40 minutes, or until knife inserted near center comes out clean. Remove from oven and spread with sour cream. return to oven and bake 5 minutes longer. Cool 15 minutes. Refrigerate 3 to 8 hours. Before serving, remove outer ring and spread top of cake with salsa, or top each serving with a scant tablespoon of salsa. Serve with taco chips, if desired.

PER SERVING: ABOUT 136 CAL, 7 g PRO, 5 g CARB, 9 g FAT, 59 mg CHOL, 421 mg SOD.

NUTTY CHEESE BALL

YIELD: 24 SERVINGS

1 cup shredded sharp Cheddar cheese

1 cup shredded Swiss cheese

1 package (8 ounces) light cream cheese

2 tablespoons chopped fresh chives

2 teaspoons Worcestershire sauce

¼ teaspoon paprika

½ teaspoon garlic powder

¼ cup finely chopped pecans

FIESTA CHEESECAKE APPETIZER

Place all ingredients except pecans in mixer bowl. Attach bowl and flat beater to mixer. Turn to Speed 4 and beat about 1 minute, or until well blended.

On waxed paper, shape mixture into a ball. Roll ball in chopped pecans. Wrap in waxed paper. Refrigerate until serving time. Serve with assorted crackers or raw vegetables.

PER SERVING: (2 TABLESPOONS) ABOUT 65 CAL, 4 g PRO, 1 g CARB, 5 g FAT, 13 mg CHOL, 109 mg SOD.

MEATBALL HORS D'OEUVRES

YIELD: 30 MEATBALLS

1 **pound ground beef**	½ **teaspoon oregano**
2 **egg yolks**	¼ **teaspoon pepper**
⅓ **cup dry bread crumbs**	2 **tablespoons chopped**
⅓ **cup Parmesan cheese**	**stuffed olives**
2 **tablespoons chopped**	¼ **cup olive oil**
parsley	**Tangy Barbecue Sauce**
¾ **teaspoon garlic salt**	**(recipe follows)**

Place ground beef, egg yolks, bread crumbs, Parmesan cheese, parsley, garlic salt, oregano, pepper, and olives in mixer bowl. Attach bowl and flat beater to mixer. Turn to Speed 2 and mix for 1 minute.

Form mixture into 30 1-inch balls and fry in olive oil until well browned. Drain on paper towels. Warm **Tangy Barbecue Sauce** and pour over meatballs. serve warm from chafing dish.

PER SERVING: ABOUT 108 CAL, 4 g PRO, 12 g CARB, 5 g FAT, 25 mg CHOL, 240 mg SOD.

TANGY BARBECUE SAUCE
YIELD: 2 CUPS

1¼ **cups brown sugar**	2 **tablespoons vinegar**
1 **cup ketchup**	1 **cup strong coffee**
1 **tablespoon dry mustard**	½ **cup finely chopped onion**
2 **tablespoons Worcestershire**	1 **teaspoon salt**
sauce	⅛ **teaspoon pepper**

Combine all ingredients in a heavy saucepan. Mix well and cook over medium heat 10 minutes, stirring occasionally. Reduce heat and simmer 30 minutes. Cool sauce and store covered in refrigerator until needed.

MUSHROOM-ONION TARTLETS

YIELD: 24 TARTLETS

4 ounces light cream cheese	**8 ounces fresh mushrooms, coarsely chopped**
3 tablespoons butter or margarine, divided	**½ cup chopped green onions**
¾ cup plus 1 teaspoon all-purpose flour	**1 egg**
	¼ cup dried thyme leaves
	½ cup shredded Swiss cheese

Place cream cheese and 2 tablespoons butter in mixer bowl. Attach bowl and flat beater to mixer. Turn to Speed 4 and beat about 1 minute. Stop and scrape bowl. Add ¾ cup flour. Turn to Speed 2 and mix about 1 minute, or until well blended. Form mixture into ball. Wrap in waxed paper and chill 1 hour. Clean mixer bowl and beater.

Divide chilled dough into 24 pieces. Press each piece into miniature muffin cup (greased, if desired).

Meanwhile, melt remaining 1 tablespoon butter in 10-inch skillet over medium heat. Add mushrooms and onions. Cook and stir until tender. Remove from heat. Cool slightly.

Place egg, remaining 1 tablespoon flour, and thyme in mixer bowl. Attach bowl and flat beater to mixer. Turn to Speed 6 and beat about 30 seconds. Stir in cheese and cooled mushroom mixture. Spoon into pastry-lined muffin cups. Bake at 375°F for 15 to 20 minutes, or until egg mixture is puffed and golden brown. Serve warm.

PER SERVING: (2 TARTLETS) ABOUT 98 CAL, 4 g PRO, 8 g CARB, 6 g FAT, 33 mg CHOL, 83 mg SOD.

ROQUEFORT NUT SPREAD

YIELD: 1½ CUPS

½ **pound Roquefort cheese, crumbled**
5 **tablespoons butter or margarine, softened**

¼ **teaspoon cayenne pepper**
1 **cup chopped walnuts**

Place cheese, butter, and cayenne pepper in mixer bowl. Attach bowl and wire whip to mixer. Turn to Speed 2 and whip 1 minute. Stop and scrape bowl. Add nuts. Turn to Speed 2 and whip 30 seconds. Serve at room temperature with assorted crackers.

PER SERVING: (2 TABLESPOONS) ABOUT 177 CAL, 56 g PRO, 2 g CARB, 17 g FAT, 30 mg CHOL, 372 mg SOD.

FRENCH ONION SOUP

YIELD: 8 SERVINGS

6 **medium onions**
¼ **pound Swiss cheese**
⅓ **cup butter or margarine**
1½ **teaspoons sugar**

6 **cups chicken or beef broth**
2 **tablespoons dry sherry**
8 **slices French bread**

Assemble Rotor Slicer/Shredder using thick slicer cone (No. 3) and attach to mixer. Turn to Speed 4 and slice onions; set aside. Exchange thick slicer cone for fine shredder cone (No. 1). Turn to Speed 4 and shred Swiss cheese; set aside.

Melt butter in large pot over medium-high heat. Add onions and sauté 15 minutes until transparent but not browned. Reduce heat and add sugar; continue cooking 20 or 25 minutes. Add broth, cover and simmer 45 minutes. Stir in sherry.

Ladle soup into individual serving bowls. Place one bread slice in each bowl ad sprinkle with Swiss cheese. Place under broiler 3 minutes or until cheese melts.

PER SERVING: ABOUT 244 CAL, 8 g PRO, 24 g CARB, 13 g FAT, 35 mg CHOL, 971 mg SOD.

ROQUEFORT NUT SPREAD

SWISS BACON CANAPÉS

YIELD: 26 APPETIZERS

¼	pound Swiss cheese	1	teaspoon Worcestershire sauce
4	slices bacon, crisply cooked and crumbled		Dash pepper
⅓	cup evaporated milk	26	2-inch bread rounds

Assemble Rotor Slicer/Shredder using fine shredder cone (No. 1) and attach to mixer. Turn to Speed 4 and shred Swiss cheese into mixer bowl. Add bacon, evaporated milk, Worcestershire sauce, and pepper. Attach bowl and flat beater to mixer. Turn to Speed 4 and beat 1 minute. Stop and scrape bowl. Turn to Speed 6 and beat 30 seconds.

Top each bread round with 1 teaspoon of cheese mixture and place on greased baking sheets. Bake at 400°F for 8 to 10 minutes or until lightly browned. Serve immediately.

PER SERVING: ABOUT 45 CAL, 2 G PRO, 4 G CARB, 2 G FAT, 6 MG CHOL, 68 MG SOD.

HERBED WHIPPED SQUASH

YIELD: 6 SERVINGS

1	large butternut squash, baked (about 3 cups cooked)	½	teaspoon dried tarragon leaves
¼	cup butter or margarine, melted	⅛	teaspoon salt
		⅛	teaspoon black pepper

Scoop cooked squash out of shell and place in mixer bowl. Attach bowl and wire whip to mixer. Turn to Speed 4 and beat about 30 seconds. Add all remaining ingredients. Turn to Speed 2 and mix about 30 seconds. Turn to Speed 4 and beat about 2 minutes.

PER SERVING: (½ CUP) ABOUT 107 CAL, 1 g PRO, 11 g CARB, 7 g FAT, 0 mg CHOL, 137 mg SOD.

SWISS BACON CANAPÉS

MAYONNAISE

YIELD: 2½ CUPS

3 **egg yolks**
2 **cups vegetable or olive oil**
1 **lemon, juiced**
1 **teaspoon salt**

¼ **teaspoon dry mustard**
1 **tablespoon cider vinegar**

Place egg yolks in mixer bowl. Attach bowl and wire whip to mixer. Turn to Speed 10 and whip about 3 minutes, or until yolks are stiff and pale yellow.

Reduce to Speed 8 and slowly add 1 cup oil, a teaspoon at a time, in a thin stream. If mixture becomes too thick, thin with a little lemon juice. Carefully add remaining oil in a slow, steady stream until completely absorbed.

Reduce to Speed 6, add lemon juice, salt, dry mustard, and vinegar, and whip just until blended. Store mayonnaise in refrigerator.

PER SERVING: (2 TABLESPOONS) ABOUT 101 CAL, 0 g PRO, 0 g CARB, 11 g FAT, 15 mg CHOL, 59 mg SOD.

TIP: If mayonnaise should separate, beat a fresh, warm egg yolk in mixer bowl for minute using the wire whip. Beat in a few drops of oil, then a teaspoon of the separated mayonnaise. As the new sauce comes together, add the separated mayonnaise in increasing amounts until all of it has been incorporated.

DILL MAYONNAISE
YIELD: 1 CUP

1 **cup mayonnaise**
1 **teaspoon dried dill weed**
1 **tablespoon lemon juice**
¼ **teaspoon pepper**

Place all ingredients in mixer bowl. Attach bowl and flat beater to mixer. Turn to Speed 2 and mix 1 minute. Chill thoroughly before serving.

PER SERVING: (2 TABLESPOONS) ABOUT 48 CAL, 0 g PRO, 2 g CARB, 4 g FAT, 6 mg CHOL, 26 mg SOD.

RUSSIAN DRESSING
YIELD: 1 1/2 CUPS

1   **cup mayonnaise**
1/2 **cup ketchup**
2   **drops hot pepper sauce**
1/4 **cup chopped parsley**
    Salt and pepper

Place all ingredients in mixer bowl. Attach bowl and flat beater to mixer. Turn to Speed 2 and mix 1 minute. Chill thoroughly before serving.

PER SERVING: (2 TABLESPOONS) ABOUT 72 CAL, 0 g PRO, 1 g CARB, 8 g FAT, 10 mg CHOL, 95 mg SOD.

BLUE CHEESE DRESSING
YIELD: 2 CUPS

1   **cup mayonnaise**
2/3 **cup crumbled blue cheese**
2   **tablespoons lemon juice**
1/4 **teaspoon pepper**

Place all ingredients in mixer bowl. Attach bowl and flat beater to mixer. Turn to Stir Speed and mix 1 minute. Chill thoroughly before servings.

PER SERVING: (2 TABLESPOONS) ABOUT 61 CAL, 1 g PRO, 0 g CARB, 6 g FAT, 10 mg CHOL, 69 mg SOD.

BROCCOLI-CHEESE BAKE

YIELD: 9 SERVINGS

1   **package (10 ounces) frozen chopped broccoli, cooked and well drained**
1   **small onion, quartered**
1/2 **pound Cheddar cheese**
1   **cup all-purpose flour**

1   **teaspoon salt**
1   **teaspoon baking powder**
1   **cup milk**
2   **eggs**
1/3 **cup butter or margarine, melted**

Assemble Food Grinder using coarse grinding plate and attach to mixer. Turn to Speed 4 and grind broccoli and onion. Set aside.

Assemble Rotor Slicer/Shredder using fine shredder cone (No. 1) and attach to mixer. Turn to Speed 4 and shred cheese. Set aside.

Sift flour, salt, and baking powder into mixer bowl. Add milk, eggs, and butter. Attach bowl and flat beater to mixer. Turn to Speed 2 and mix 1 minute.

Add broccoli mixture and cheese. Turn to Speed 2 and mix 30 seconds. Pour mixture into greased 9-inch square pan. Bake at 375°F for 60 to 75 minutes. Cut into 3-inch squares to serve.

PER SERVING: ABOUT 256 CAL, 11 g PRO, 15 g CARB, 17 g FAT, 94 mg CHOL, 554 mg SOD.

CRABMEAT DIP

YIELD: 24 SERVINGS

1 package (8 ounces) light cream cheese
1 cup reduced-fat cottage cheese
¼ cup reduced-calorie mayonnaise
1 can (6½ ounces) crabmeat, flaked
1 tablespoon lemon juice
3 tablespoons chopped green onions
½ teaspoon garlic salt
3 drops hot pepper sauce

Place cream cheese, cottage cheese, and mayonnaise in mixer bowl. Attach bowl and flat beater to mixer. Turn to Speed 6 and beat about 1 minute, or until well blended. Stop and scrape bowl. Add all remaining ingredients. Turn to Speed 6 and beat 1 minute, or until all ingredients are combined.

Refrigerate until well chilled. Serve with assorted crackers or raw vegetables.

PER SERVING: (2 TABLESPOONS) ABOUT 42 CAL, 4 g PRO, 1 g CARB, 3 g FAT, 12 mg CHOL, 180 mg SOD.

HUMMUS

YIELD: 2 CUPS

1 can (20 ounces) chickpeas, drained
¼ cup cold water
¼ cup fresh lemon juice
¼ cup tahini (sesame seed paste)
3 cloves garlic, minced
½ teaspoon salt
¼ teaspoon paprika (optional)

Assemble Fruit/Vegetable Strainer and attach to mixer. Turn to Speed 4 and strain chickpeas into mixer bowl. Return waste to strained chickpeas.

Add water, lemon juice, tahini, garlic, salt, and paprika. Attach bowl and wire whip to mixer. Turn to Speed 4 and whip 1 minute. Stop and scrape bowl. Increase to Speed 10 and whip 1 minute or until smooth. Serve with **Pita Bread** (see page 35).

PER SERVING: (2 TABLESPOONS) ABOUT 66 CAL, 2 g PRO, 9 g CARB, 2 g FAT, 0 mg CHOL, 180 mg SOD.

SPINACH AND CHEESE CROSTINI

YIELD: 24 CROSTINI

1 **baguette loaf, cut into ½-inch slices**
2 **teaspoons butter or margarine**
½ **cup finely chopped onion**
1 **clove garlic, minced**

1 **package (9 ounces) frozen chopped spinach, thawed and squeezed dry**
1 **package (8 ounces) light cream cheese**
¼ **cup roasted red peppers**
½ **cup shredded Cheddar cheese**

Place baguette slices on baking sheet. Bake at 375°F for 4 to 6 minutes, or until toasted. Set aside.

Melt butter in 10-inch skillet over medium heat. Add onion and garlic. Cook and stir 2 to 3 minutes, or until softened. Add spinach. Cook and stir 30 to 60 seconds, or until warm. Cool slightly.

Place cream cheese in mixer bowl. Attach bowl and flat beater to mixer. Turn to Speed 2, mix about 30 seconds. Add spinach mixture. Continuing on Speed 2, mix about 30 seconds. Add red peppers. Continuing on Speed 2, mix about 30 seconds. Spread spinach mixture on toasted baguette slices. Top each slice with about 1 teaspoon Cheddar cheese. Bake 375°F for 5 to 8 minutes, or until thoroughly heated and cheese is melted. Serve warm.

PER SERVING: **(2 CROSTINI) ABOUT 141 CAL, 6 g PRO, 16 g CARB, 6 g FAT, 12 mg CHOL, 324 mg SOD.**

MASHED POTATOES

YIELD: 9 SERVINGS

5 large potatoes (about 2½ pounds), peeled, quartered, and boiled	**2 tablespoons butter or margarine**
½ cup low-fat milk, heated	**1 teaspoon salt**
	⅛ teaspoon black pepper

Warm mixer bowl and flat beater with hot water; dry. Place hot potatoes in bowl. Attach bowl and flat beater to mixer. Gradually turn to Speed 2 and mix until smooth, about 1 minute.

Add all remaining ingredients. Turn to Speed 4 and beat about until milk is absorbed, about 30 seconds. Gradually turn to Speed 6 and beat until fluffy, about 1 minute. Stop and scrape bowl. Exchange flat beater for wire whip. Turn to Speed 10 and whip 2 to 3 minutes.

PER SERVING: (¾ CUP) ABOUT 119 CAL, 3 g PRO, 20 g CARB, 3 g FAT, 8 mg CHOL, 300 mg SOD.

GARLIC MASHED POTATOES:
Substitute 1 teaspoon garlic salt for salt.

PER SERVING: ABOUT 119 CAL, 3 g PRO, 20 g CARB, 3 g FAT, 8 mg CHOL, 149 mg SOD.

PARMESAN MASHED POTATOES:
Increase milk to ¾ cup. Add ⅓ cup grated Parmesan cheese with milk.

PER SERVING: ABOUT 136 CAL, 4 g PRO, 21 g CARB, 4 g FAT, 11 mg CHOL, 359 mg SOD.

SOUR CREAM-CHIVE MASHED POTATOES: Substitute ¼ cup reduced-fat sour cream for ¼ cup milk. Add 2 tablespoons chopped fresh chives.

PER SERVING: ABOUT 127 CAL, 3 g PRO, 20 g CARB, 4 g FAT, 10 mg CHOL, 300 mg SOD.

POTATO PANCAKES

YIELD: 6 SERVINGS

3 medium potatoes, peeled
   and halved
1 small onion
3 eggs
2 tablespoons all-purpose
   flour

1 tablespoon chopped parsley
1 teaspoon salt
Dash pepper
Vegetable oil for frying

Assemble Rotor Slicer/Shredder using fine shredder cones (No. 1) and attach to mixer. Turn to Speed 4 and shred potatoes and onion.

Place eggs in mixer bowl. Attach bowl and flat beater to mixer. Turn to Speed 2 and beat 1 minute. Add potatoes, onion, flour, salt, parsley, and pepper. Turn to Stir Speed and mix until well blended, about 30 seconds.

Heat a small amount of oil in a 12-inch skillet over medium heat. Drop 3 tablespoons of potato mixture for each pancake into hot oil. Fry until golden brown, about 4 to 5 minutes per side. Serve immediately.

PER SERVING: ABOUT 113 CAL, 5 g PRO, 18 g CARB, 3 g FAT, 106 mg CHOL, 427 mg SOD.

POPPY SEED DRESSING

YIELD: 1½ CUPS

¼ cup sugar
⅓ cup cider vinegar
1 teaspoon dry mustard
1 teaspoon minced onion

1 teaspoon salt
1 cup vegetable oil
1½ teaspoons poppy seeds

Place sugar, vinegar, dry mustard, onion, and salt in mixer bowl. Attach bowl and wire whip to mixer. Turn to Speed 4 and whip 2 minutes.

Increase to Speed 8 and slowly add oil in a thin, steady stream until completely absorbed. Reduce to Stir Speed and add poppy seeds, mixing just until combined. Chill thoroughly before serving.

PER SERVING: (2 TABLESPOONS) ABOUT 90 CAL, 0 g PRO, 2 g CARB, 9 g FAT, 0 mg CHOL, 97 mg SOD.

Essential BREADS

Your KitchenAid® Stand Mixer

makes *baking* homemade

bread simple, whether turning

out braided loaves for special

occasions or muffins for

weekday mornings.

POPOVERS
(page 34)

POPOVERS

Pictured on page 33

YIELD: 8 POPOVERS

2 eggs	**1 cup all-purpose flour**
1 cup milk	**¼ teaspoon salt**
1 tablespoon butter or margarine, melted	

Place eggs, milk, butter, flour, and salt in mixer bowl. Attach bowl and wire whip to mixer. Turn to Speed 4 and beat 15 seconds. Stop and scrape bowl. Turn to Speed 4 and beat 15 seconds more.

Fill 8 heavily greased and floured custard cups half full with batter. Place cups on cookie sheet. Place cookie sheet in cold oven and set heat at 450°F. Bake for 15 minutes; reduce heat to 350°F and bake 20 to 25 minutes longer. Remove from oven and cut slit into side of each popover. Serve immediately.

PER SERVING: ABOUT 103 CAL, 4 g PRO, 13 g CARB, 3 g FAT, 59 mg CHOL, 115 mg SOD.

RAISIN-WHEAT MUFFINS

YIELD: 18 MUFFINS

1¾ cups wheat berries or 2 cups whole wheat flour	**⅓ cup honey**
2 eggs	**⅓ cup vegetable oil**
⅓ cup yogurt	**¾ teaspoon salt**
⅔ cups warm milk (105°F to 115°F)	**1 teaspoon baking soda**
	⅓ cup raisins

Assemble Grain Mill and attach to mixer. Set Mill on Click 3. Turn to Speed 10 and grind berries into whole wheat flour. Set aside.

Place eggs in mixer bowl. Attach bowl and wire whip to mixer. Turn to Speed 2 and beat 15 seconds. Add yogurt and milk. Turn to Speed 4 and beat 15 seconds.

Add honey, oil, flour, salt, baking soda, and raisins. Turn to Speed 2 and mix until well blended, about 15 seconds.

Pour batter into ungreased muffin tins. Bake at 425°F for 15 minutes.

PER SERVING: ABOUT 131 CAL, 3 g PRO, 18 g CARB, 6 g FAT, 24 mg CHOL, 183 mg SOD.

PITA BREAD

YIELD: 6 LOAVES

1¾ **cups wheat berries or
 2 cups whole wheat flour**
3½ **cups all-purpose flour**
 1 **tablespoon sugar**

2 **teaspoons salt**
1 **package active dry yeast**
2 **cups very warm water
 (120°F to 130°F)**

Assemble Grain Mill and attach to mixer. Set Mill on Click 3. Turn to Speed 10 and grind berries into whole wheat flour. Set aside.

Mix flours together. Place 4 cups flour mixture, sugar, salt, and yeast in mixer bowl. Attach bowl and dough hook to mixer. Turn to Speed 2 and mix 15 seconds. Gradually add warm water and mix 1 minute. Continuing on Speed 2, add remaining flour mixture, ½ cup at a time, until dough clings to hook and cleans sides of bowl. Knead on Speed 2 for 2 minutes longer, or until dough is smooth and elastic.

Place in greased bowl, turning to grease top. cover; let rise in warm place, free from draft, until doubled in bulk about 1 hour.

Punch dough down and divide into six equal pieces. Roll each piece into 7-inch circle. Place circles on aluminum foil and let rise, uncovered, at room temperature for 1 hour.

Bake circles individually on foil at 500°F for 5 to 6 minutes. Remove from foil immediately and cool on wire racks.

PER SERVING: **ABOUT 418 CAL, 14 g PRO, 83 g CARB, 3 g FAT, 0 mg CHOL, 777 mg SOD.**

ORANGE MUFFINS

⅓ **cup butter or margarine**
½ **cup sugar**
1 **egg**
1 **teaspoon grated orange peel**
½ **cup orange juice**

¼ **cup milk**
2 **cups all-purpose flour**
2 **teaspoons baking powder**
½ **teaspoon baking soda**
½ **teaspoon salt**

Place butter and sugar in mixer bowl. Attach bowl and flat beater to mixer. Turn to Speed 6 and beat 1 minute. Stop and scrape bowl. Add egg, orange peel, orange juice, and milk. Turn to Speed 4 and beat 30 seconds.

Combine flour, baking powder, baking soda, and salt, and add to bowl. Turn to Speed 2 and mix 15 seconds, or just until moistened. Do not overbeat.

Fill greased muffin tins two-thirds full. Bake at 400°F for 20 to 25 minutes. Serve warm.

PER SERVING: **ABOUT 166 CAL, 3 g PRO, 25 g CARB, 6 g FAT, 32 mg CHOL, 276 mg SOD.**

BAKING POWDER BISCUITS

YIELD: 12 BISCUITS

2	**cups all-purpose flour**	**⅓**	**cup shortening**
4	**teaspoons baking powder**	**⅔**	**cup low-fat milk**
½	**teaspoon salt**		**Melted butter or margarine, if desired**

Place flour, baking powder, salt, and shortening in mixer bowl. Attach bowl and flat beater to mixer. Turn to Stir Speed and mix about 1 minute. Stop and scrape bowl.

Continuing on Stir Speed, add milk and mix until dough starts to cling to beater. Do not overbeat. Turn dough onto lightly floured surface and knead about 20 seconds, or until smooth. Pat or roll to ½-inch thickness. Cut with floured 2-inch biscuit cutter.

Place on greased baking sheets and brush with melted butter, if desired. Bake at 450°F for 12 to 15 minutes. Serve immediately.

PER SERVING: **ABOUT 135 CAL, 3 g PRO, 17 g CARB, 6 g FAT, 1 mg CHOL, 183 mg SOD.**

LEMON TEA BREAD

YIELD: 1 LOAF

½ **cup butter or margarine, softened**	¼ **teaspoon salt**
1 **cup sugar**	⅓ **cup milk**
2 **eggs**	½ **cup chopped walnuts**
2 **cups all-purpose flour**	2 **tablespoons grated lemon peel**
1½ **teaspoons baking powder**	**Lemon Glaze (recipe follows)**

Place butter, sugar, and eggs in mixer bowl. Attach bowl and flat beater to mixer. Turn to Speed 6 and beat 1 minute. Stop and scrape bowl.

Combine flour, baking powder, and salt. Turn to Speed 2 and add one third of the flour mixture alternately with half the milk, beating 15 seconds after each addition. Repeat until all ingredients are used. Stop and scrape bowl. Turn to Stir Speed and quickly add walnuts and lemon peel.

Pour batter into greased 8½×4½×2½-inch loaf pan. Bake at 325°F for 55 to 65 minutes. Brush with **Lemon Glaze** and cool in pan 15 minutes; remove and cool on wire rack.

LEMON GLAZE
YIELD: ¼ CUP

¼ **cup fresh lemon juice**
3 **tablespoons sugar**

Place lemon juice and sugar in small saucepan. Bring to a boil over medium heat and stir until slightly thickened. Remove from heat.

PER SERVING: (¹⁄₁₆ **LOAF) ABOUT 201 CAL, 3 g PRO, 28 g CARB, 9 g FAT, 42 mg CHOL, 135 mg SOD.**

SCONES

2 **cups all-purpose flour**
2 **tablespoons sugar**
2 **teaspoons baking powder**
½ **teaspoon salt**

⅓ **cup butter or margarine, softened**
2 **eggs**
½ **cup heavy cream**
1 **teaspoon water**

Place flour, sugar, baking powder, salt, and butter in mixer bowl. Attach bowl and flat beater to mixer. Turn to Speed 2 and beat 30 seconds or until well blended. Stop and scrape bowl.

Add 1 egg and cream. Turn to Speed 2 and beat 30 seconds or until soft dough forms. Knead dough three times on lightly floured surface. Divide dough in half. Pat each half into circle about ½-inch thick. Cut each circle into eight wedges.

Place wedges 2 inches apart on greased baking sheets. Beat remaining egg and water together. Brush egg mixture over each wedge. Bake at 425°F for 10 to 12 minutes. Serve immediately.

PER SERVING: **ABOUT 132 CAL, 3 g PRO, 14 g CARB, 7 g FAT, 47 mg CHOL, 173 mg SOD.**

GARLIC PULL-APART BREAD

YIELD: 2 LOAVES

6 to 7 cups all-purpose flour, divided	**2 packages active dry yeast**
3 tablespoons sugar	**1½ cups water**
2 tablespoons garlic salt, divided	**½ cup milk**
	½ cup (1 stick) butter or margarine, divided

Place 5 cups flour, sugar, 1 tablespoon garlic salt, and yeast in mixer bowl. Attach bowl and dough hook to mixer. Turn to Speed 2 and mix 15 seconds. Combine water, milk, and ¼ cup butter in small saucepan. Heat over low heat until liquids are very warm (120°F to 130°F).

Turn to Speed 2 and gradually add warm liquids to flour mixture, about 30 seconds. Mix 1 minute longer. Continuing on Speed 2, add remaining flour, ½ cup at a time, until dough clings to hook and cleans sides of bowl. Knead on Speed 2 for 2 minutes longer.

Place in a greased bowl, turning to grease top. Cover; let rise in warm place, free from draft, until doubled in bulk, about 1 hour.

Punch dough down and divide in half. Roll one half into 12×8×¼-inch rectangle. Melt remaining butter and mix with remaining garlic salt. Brush dough with mixture. Cut dough into four equal 8×3-inch strips. Stack strips and cut into four equal 3×2-inch strips. Place pieces on edge in greased 8½×4½×2½-inch loaf pan so strips form one row down length of pan. Repeat with remaining dough. Cover; let rise in warm place, free from draft, until doubled in bulk, about 1 hour. Bake at 400°F for 30 to 35 minutes. Remove from pans immediately and cool on wire racks.

PER SERVING: (¹⁄₁₆ **LOAF) ABOUT 119 CAL, 3 g PRO, 20 g CARB, 3 g FAT, 8 mg CHOL, 297 mg SOD.**

BOURBON STREET BEIGNETS

YIELD: 5 DOZEN DOUGHNUTS

¼ **cup warm water (105°F to 115°F)**
1 **package active dry yeast**
¼ **cup granulated sugar**
2 **tablespoons shortening**
½ **teaspoon salt**
½ **cup boiling water**

½ **cup heavy cream**
1 **egg, beaten**
4 **to 4½ cups all-purpose flour, divided**
Oil for deep frying
Powdered sugar

Dissolve yeast in warm water; set aside. Place granulated sugar, shortening, salt, and boiling water in mixer bowl. Stir until shortening is melted and sugar dissolves; cool to lukewarm. Add cream, egg, 3 cups flour and yeast. Attach bowl and dough hook to mixer. Turn to Speed 2 and mix 2 minutes. Add remaining flour ½ cup at a time, until dough clings to hook and cleans sides of bowl, about 2 minutes. Knead on Speed 2 for 2 minutes longer.

Place dough on lightly floured board and roll into 10×24-inch rectangle. Using sharp knife, cut dough into 2-inch squares.

Pour oil into large heavy saucepan or deep fryer to a depth of 2 inches then heat oil to 360°F. Fry doughnuts, four at a time, turning to brown on both sides, about 3 minutes. Drain on paper towels and sprinkle with powdered sugar.

PER SERVING: **ABOUT 46 CAL, 1 g PRO, 7 g CARB, 1 g FAT, 6 mg CHOL, 22 mg SOD.**

NOTE: Doughnuts can be filled with custard, whipping cream, or jelly using a small pastry tube.

PANETTONE

4 to 4½ cups all-purpose flour, divided	1 cup warm milk (105°F to 115°F)
1 teaspoon salt	½ cup vegetable oil
½ cup raisins	¼ cup (½ stick) butter or margarine, melted
1 teaspoon grated lemon peel	
½ cup chopped candied citron	4 egg yolks, beaten
¼ cup sugar	1 egg white
1 package active dry yeast	1 tablespoon water

Place 3 cups flour, salt, raisins, lemon peel, candied citron, and sugar in mixer bowl. Attach bowl and dough hook to mixer. Turn to Speed 2 and mix 15 seconds. Dissolve yeast in warm milk, then add oil and butter.

Turn to Speed 2 and gradually add warm milk mixture and egg yolks to flour mixture. Mix 1 minute. Continuing on Speed 2, add remaining flour, ½ cup at a time, until dough clings to hook* and cleans sides of bowl. Knead on Speed 2 for 2 minutes longer.

*NOTE: Dough may not form a ball on hook; however, as long as there is contact between dough and hook, kneading will be accomplished. Do not add more than the maximum amount of flour specified or dry loaf will result.

Place in greased bowl, turning to grease top. Cover; let rise in warm place, free from draft, until doubled in bulk, about 1 hour.

Punch dough down and shape into ball. Place in greased and floured 1½-quart soufflé dish. Let rise, uncovered, in warm place, free from draft, until doubled in bulk, about 1 hour.

Cut two slashes with a sharp knife in a cross pattern on top of loaf. Beat egg white and water together with a fork and brush top of loaf with mixture. Bake at 350°F for 55 to 60 minutes. Remove from baking dish immediately and cool on wire rack.

PER SERVING: (¹⁄₁₆ **LOAF) ABOUT 266 CAL, 5 g PRO, 36 g CARB, 11 g FAT, 60 mg CHOL, 184 mg SOD.**

RUSSIAN BLACK BREAD

YIELD: 1 LOAF

¾ **cup rye berries or 1 cup rye flour**
2 **tablespoons vinegar**
2 **tablespoons dark molasses**
½ **ounce (½ square) unsweetened chocolate**
2 **tablespoons butter or margarine**
1 **cup water, divided**
1 **package active dry yeast**

2 **cups all-purpose flour**
½ **cup bran cereal**
2 **teaspoons caraway seeds**
½ **teaspoon sugar**
1 **teaspoon salt**
½ **teaspoon instant coffee**
½ **teaspoon onion powder**
½ **teaspoon cornstarch**

Assemble Grain Mill and attach to mixer. Set Mill on Click 3. Turn to Speed 10 and grind rye berries into rye flour. Set aside.

Heat vinegar, molasses, and chocolate in small saucepan over medium heat until chocolate melts. Stir in butter and cool to lukewarm.

Heat ¾ cup water to 105°F to 115°F. Dissolve yeast in warm water.

Mix flours together. Place 2 cups flour mixture, cereal, caraway seeds, sugar, salt, coffee, and onion powder in mixer bowl. Attach bowl and dough hook to mixer. Turn to Speed 2 and mix 15 seconds. Continuing on Speed 2, gradually add yeast mixture and warm liquids in thin, steady stream, taking about 1 minute. Add remaining flour mixture, ½ cup at a time until dough clings to hook* and cleans sides of bowl. Knead on Speed 2 for 2 minutes or until smooth and elastic.

*NOTE: Dough may not form a ball on hook; however, as long as there is contact between dough and hook, kneading will be accomplished. Do not add more than the maximum amount of flour specified or dry loaf will result.

Place in greased bowl, turning to grease top. Cover; let rise in warm place, free from draft, until doubled in bulk, about 1 hour.

Punch dough down and shape into round loaf. Place in greased 8-inch cake pan. Cover; let rise in warm place, free from draft, until doubled in bulk, about 1 hour.

Bake at 350°F for 35 to 40 minutes. Combine remaining ¼ cup water and cornstarch in small saucepan over medium heat. Stir constantly until mixture comes to a boil and cook for 30 seconds. Brush cornstarch mixture over loaf and return to oven for 2 minutes. Remove from pan immediately and cool on wire rack.

PER SERVING: (¹⁄₁₆ **LOAF) ABOUT 112 CAL, 3 g PRO, 20 g CARB, 3 g FAT, 4 mg CHOL, 162 mg SOD.**

GERMAN APPLE PANCAKES

YIELD: 12 TO 16 PANCAKES

1 **cup all-purpose flour**	2 **teaspoons baking powder**
1 **cup diced, peeled apple**	¼ **teaspoon salt**
¾ **cup milk**	⅛ **teaspoon cinnamon**
1 **egg**	**Dash ground cloves**
2 **tablespoons sugar**	

Place all ingredients in mixer bowl. Attach bowl and wire whip to mixer. Turn to Speed 6 and whip 30 seconds. Stop and scrape bowl. Turn to Speed 6 and whip 15 seconds, or until smooth.

Slowly heat greased griddle or heavy skillet over medium-high heat. Drop batter by 2 tablespoonfuls onto griddle. Cook until bubbles form on surface and edges become dry. Turn and cook until golden brown on underside. Serve immediately.

PER SERVING: **ABOUT 65 CAL, 2 g PRO, 12 g CARB, 1 g FAT, 19 mg CHOL, 143 mg SOD.**

SOUR CREAM SODA BREAD

YIELD: 1 LOAF

2 **cups all-purpose flour**	½ **cup raisins**
¾ **teaspoon baking soda**	1 **tablespoon caraway seeds**
½ **teaspoon salt**	1 **cup sour cream**
3 **tablespoons sugar**	1 **tablespoon milk**
½ **cup (1 stick) butter or margarine, softened**	

Place flour, soda, salt, sugar, and butter in bowl. Attach bowl and flat beater to mixer. Turn to Speed 4 and mix 2 minutes or until mixture is crumbly. Stop and scrape bowl.

Add raisins, caraway seeds, and sour cream. Turn to Speed 2 and beat 1 minute or until well blended. Form dough into a mound-shaped circle on greased baking sheet. Brush dough with milk. Bake at 375°F for 45 to 55 minutes. Remove from baking sheet and cool on wire rack.

PER SERVING: (¹⁄₁₆ **LOAF) ABOUT 159 CAL, 2 g PRO, 19 g CARB, 9 g FAT, 21 mg CHOL, 180 mg SOD.**

APPLE CRUMB COFFEE CAKE

YIELD: 1 COFFEE CAKE

½ **cup milk**
¼ **cup (½ stick) butter or margarine**
¼ **cup warm water (105°F to 115°F)**
3 **to 3½ cups all-purpose flour, divided**
¼ **cup sugar**

1 **teaspoon salt**
1 **package active dry yeast**
1 **egg**
Cinnamon Crumb Filling (recipe follows)
2 **apples, peeled, cored and thinly sliced**

Scald milk; add butter and water. Cool to lukewarm. Place 2 cups flour, sugar, salt, and yeast in mixer bowl. Attach bowl and dough hook to mixer. Turn to Speed 2 and mix 15 seconds. Gradually add warm liquid to bowl, mixing 1 minute. Add egg and mix 1 minute longer. Continuing on Speed 2, add remaining flour, ½ cup at a time, until dough clings to hook and cleans sides of bowl. Knead on Speed 2 for 2 minutes longer.

Place in greased bowl, turning to grease top. Cover; let rise in warm place, free from draft, until doubled in bulk, about 1 hour.

Punch down dough and divide in half. Roll each half to 9 inch circle. Place one circle in bottom of greased 9-inch springform pan. Sprinkle one quarter of **Cinnamon Crumb Filling** over dough. Arrange half the apple slices on filling; sprinkle another quarter filling over apples. Place remaining dough circle in pan and repeat layers with remaining crumb mixture and apples. Cover; let rise in warm place, free from draft, until doubled in bulk, about 1 hour.

Bake at 375°F for 45 to 50 minutes. Remove sides of springform pan immediately and cool on wire rack.

CINNAMON CRUMB FILLING

1 **cup sugar**
¾ **cup all-purpose flour**

2½ **teaspoons cinnamon**
6 **tablespoons butter**

Mix all ingredients with fork until crumbly.

PER SERVING: (¹⁄₁₆ **CAKE) ABOUT 331 CAL, 5 g PRO, 54 g CARB, 11 g FAT, 44 mg CHOL, 274 mg SOD.**

CHEESE BRAID

YIELD: 2 LOAVES

1	**cup milk**	**2**	**teaspoons salt**
¼	**cup water**	**2**	**packages active dry yeast**
4	**to 4½ cups all-purpose flour, divided**	**2**	**cups shredded Cheddar cheese**
2	**tablespoons sugar**		

Heat milk and water in small saucepan over medium heat until liquids are very warm (120°F to 130°F). Place 3 cups flour, sugar, salt, and yeast in mixer bowl. Attach bowl and dough hook to mixer. Turn to Speed 2 and mix 15 seconds. Gradually add warm liquids to bowl, about 30 seconds. Continue mixing an additional minute. Add cheese and mix 1 minute.

Continuing on Speed 2, add remaining flour, ½ cup at a time, until dough clings to hook and cleans sides of bowl. Knead on Speed 2 for 2 minutes longer, or until dough is smooth and elastic.

Place in greased bowl, turning to grease top. Cover; let rise in warm place, free from draft, until doubled in bulk, about 1 hour.

Punch dough down and divide into six equal pieces. Roll each piece into a 14-inch rope. Braid three ropes together, tucking ends under, to form one loaf. Place on greased baking sheet. Repeat with remaining ropes. Cover; let rise in warm place, free from draft, until doubled in bulk, about 45 minutes.

Bake at 375°F for 20 to 25 minutes. remove from baking sheets immediately and cool on wire racks.

PER SERVING: (¹⁄₁₆ **LOAF) ABOUT 124 CAL, 5 g PRO, 18 g CARB, 4 g FAT, 11 mg CHOL, 258 mg SOD.**

BRIOCHE RING

2 packages active dry yeast	**9 tablespoons sugar, divided**
1 cup warm milk (105°F to 115°F)	**1 teaspoon salt**
3¾ to 4¼ cups unbleached flour, divided	**3 eggs**
¾ cup butter or margarine, softened	**2 egg yolks, divided**
	2 tablespoons milk
	3 tablespoons chopped pecans

Sponge: Dissolve yeast in warm milk in a medium bowl. Add 1¾ cups flour and mix thoroughly. Cover bowl with plastic wrap and allow mixture to rise 45 minutes.

Dough: Place butter, 6 tablespoons sugar, and salt in mixer bowl. Attach bowl and flat beater to mixer. Turn to Speed 4 and cream ingredients 1 minute. Stop and scrape bowl. Turn to Speed 2 and add eggs and 1 egg yolk, one at a time, beating 15 seconds after each addition.

Exchange beater for dough hook and add 1¾ cups flour. Turn to Speed 2 and mix 1 minute until well combined. Continuing on Speed 2, add remaining flour, ¼ cup at a time, until dough clings to hook and cleans sides of bowl.

Add sponge to dough. Turn to Speed 2 and knead 3 minutes. Sponge should knead into dough completely within 3 minutes.

Place dough in greased bowl, turning to grease top. Cover; let rise at room temperature, until doubled in bulk, about 2 hours. Punch dough down. Cover bowl with plastic wrap and refrigerate at least 4 hours or overnight.

Punch dough down and divide in half. Shape one half into ball. Poke hole through center of ball and gently widen by stretching dough. Continue stretching to make doughnut-shaped ring 8 to 9 inches in diameter. Place ring on greased baking sheet. Place 1½-pint bowl, the outside of which has been well greased, upside down in center of ring to prevent hole from closing during baking. Repeat with remaining dough. Cover; let rise in warm place, free from draft, until doubled in bulk, about 1 hour.

Beat remaining egg yolk and milk together. Brush mixture on each ring and sprinkle with chopped nuts and remaining sugar. Bake at 350°F for 30 to 35 minutes. remove from baking sheets immediately and cool on wire racks.

PER SERVING: (¹⁄₁₆ **LOAF) ABOUT 166 CAL, 4 g PRO, 20 g CARB, 8 g FAT, 60 mg CHOL, 153 mg SOD.**

Extraordinary ENTREÉS

Your KitchenAid® Stand Mixer

is more than a baker's best friend,

making entreés like homemade

pasta, osso bucco, and shrimp

gumbo as *easy* as

you please.

BRAISED LAMB MEDITERRANEAN

(page 58)

BRAISED LAMB MEDITERRANEAN

Pictured on page 57

YIELD: 4 SERVINGS

2 carrots, peeled	**1 clove garlic, minced**
1 large onion, halved	**½ cup dry white wine**
¼ pound fresh green beans	**½ cup water**
¼ cup all-purpose flour	**1 can (6 ounces) tomato paste**
1 teaspoon salt	**3 tablespoons chopped fresh dill**
¼ teaspoon pepper	
3 pounds lamb chops or shanks	**2 tablespoons chopped parsley**
2 tablespoons olive oil	**1 teaspoon oregano**

Assemble Rotor Slicer/Shredder using coarse shredder cone (No. 2) and attach to mixer. Turn to Speed 4 and shred carrots. Exchange coarse shredder for thick slicer cone (No. 3). Turn to Speed 4 and slice onions and green beans. Set aside.

Combine flour, salt, and pepper; dredge meat in flour mixture. Heat olive oil in a 12-inch skillet over medium heat. Brown meat on all sides. Remove from pan and drain excess oil. Add carrots, onions, green beans, and garlic. Sauté 2 minutes.

Place vegetables in a greased 13×9×2-inch pan. Arrange meat on top. Combine white wine, water, tomato paste, parsley, and oregano. Pour over meat and vegetables. Cover tightly and bake at 350°F for 2 hours, or until meat is tender. Serve immediately.

PER SERVING: ABOUT 521 CAL, 62 g PRO, 22 g CARB, 18 g FAT, 177 mg CHOL, 1125 mg SOD.

OSSO BUCO

1 **large onion, cut into sixths**	½ **cup olive oil, divided**
2 **carrots, peeled and cut into 1-inch pieces**	6 **pounds veal shanks, cut into 2½-inch lengths**
2 **stalks celery, cut into 1-inch pieces**	1 **cup dry white wine**
2 **cloves garlic**	2 **cans (28 ounces each) Italian tomatoes, seeded and coarsely chopped with juice reserved**
¼ **cup (½ stick) butter or margarine**	
1 **tablespoon lemon peel**	½ **teaspoon basil**
1 **cup all-purpose flour**	¼ **teaspoon thyme**
¼ **teaspoon salt**	2 **bay leaves**
⅛ **teaspoon pepper**	3 **sprigs parsley**

Assemble Food Grinder using coarse grinding plate and attach to mixer. Turn to Speed 4 and grind onion, carrot, celery, and garlic. Melt butter in a large Dutch oven or roaster over medium heat. Add ground vegetables and sauté 5 minutes, or until tender. Remove from heat and stir in lemon peel.

Combine flour, salt, and pepper; dredge meat in flour mixture. Heat half of oil in a 12-inch skillet. Brown half of meat until golden brown. Add remaining oil and brown remaining meat. Place meat, cut side up, on vegetables in Dutch oven.

Drain fat from skillet and add wine. Boil 1 to 2 minutes, scraping up the cooking residues from the bottom of the pan. Pour mixture over meat.

Combine tomatoes and reserved juice, basil, thyme, bay leaves, and parsley. Pour over meat and bring mixture to a simmer over medium heat. Bake in lower third of oven at 350°F for 1½ to 2 hours, or until meat is tender.

PER SERVING: ABOUT 775 CAL, 66 g PRO, 34 g CARB, 34 g FAT, 258 mg CHOL, 1102 mg SOD.

BLACK BEAN FRITTATA

YIELD: 6 SERVINGS

2 cups fat-free egg substitute or 8 eggs	**4** green onions, sliced
¼ cup low-fat milk	**1** can (16 ounces) black beans, rinsed and drained
1 tablespoon oil	**1** cup shredded Monterey Jack cheese
½ medium red bell pepper, chopped	

Place egg substitute and milk in mixer bowl. Attach bowl and wire whip to mixer. Turn to Speed 2 and mix about 30 seconds. Set aside.

Heat oil in large skillet over medium heat until oil sizzles. Add bell pepper and onions. Cook about 1 minute, or until slightly tender. Stir in beans. Cook about 1 minute, or until thoroughly heated.

Reduce heat to medium-low. Pour egg mixture over vegetables. Cook about 6 minutes, or until almost set. As bottom of egg mixture sets, carefully lift edges with spatula and let uncooked egg run to the bottom of the pan. Cook, covered, about 2 minutes, or until top is set but shiny. Sprinkle with cheese. Cook covered, about 1 minute, or until cheese melts.

PER SERVING: ABOUT 208 CAL, 18 g PRO, 15 g CARB, 8 g FAT, 18 mg CHOL, 463 mg SOD.

TIP: For browned top on frittata, place under broiler about 1 minute, or until cheese is browned and bubbly.

BOLOGNESE SAUCE

YIELD: 2 QUARTS

2 **tablespoons olive oil**	6 **large ripe tomatoes, cut into sixths**
2 **carrots, peeled and cut into 1-inch pieces**	1 **teaspoon basil**
2 **stalks celery cut into 1-inch pieces**	1 **teaspoon oregano**
1 **large onion, cut into eigths**	1 **bay leaf**
¼ **cup parsley sprigs**	1½ **teaspoons salt**
1½ **pounds ground beef**	¼ **teaspoon pepper**
½ **pound ground pork**	¼ **cup water**
3 **cloves garlic**	¼ **cup dry red wine**

Heat oil in a 12-inch skillet over medium heat. Add carrots, celery, onion, parsley, ground beef, ground pork, and garlic. Sauté 20 minutes. Remove mixture from heat and cool 10 minutes.

Assemble Food Grinder using coarse grinding plate and attach to mixer. Turn to Speed 4 and grind mixture into a 6-quart pot.

Assemble Fruit/Vegetable Strainer and attach to mixer. Turn to Speed 4 and strain tomatoes. Measure out 4 cups puree. Add tomato puree, basil, oregano, bay leaf, salt, pepper, tomato paste, water, and wine to meat mixture. Cover and simmer on medium-low heat for 1 hour.

PER SERVING: (½ **CUP) ABOUT 330 CAL, 22 g PRO, 8 g CARB, 23 g FAT, 77 mg CHOL, 534 mg SOD.**

CHEESE-STUFFED SHELLS

YIELD: 4 TO 6 SERVINGS

½ **cup fat-free egg substitute or 2 eggs**

1 **container (15 ounces) non-fat ricotta cheese**

2 **cups shredded part-skim mozzarella**

¼ **cup grated Parmesan cheese**

2 **teaspoons dried parsley leaves**

2 **teaspoons no-salt herb and garlic seasoning mix**

24 **jumbo pasta shells, cooked and drained**

2 **cups prepared marinara sauce**

Place egg substitute, ricotta cheese, mozzarella cheese, Parmesan cheese, parsley, and seasoning mix in mixer bowl. Attach bowl and flat beater to mixer. Turn to Speed 2 and mix about 30 seconds, or until combined.

Fill each shell with 2 to 3 tablespoons cheese mixture. Place filled shells in 13×9×2-inch baking pan. Pour marinara sauce over shells. Cover pan with foil. Bake at 350°F for 30 to 35 minutes, or until bubbly.

PER SERVING: ABOUT 527 CAL, 46 g PRO, 56 g CARB, 15 g FAT, 57 mg CHOL, 865 mg SOD.

CHICKEN AND MUSHROOM CASEROLE

YIELD: 4 SERVINGS

2 **tablespoons butter or margarine**

3 **boneless, skinless chicken breast halves, cut into ½-inch pieces**

1 **medium onion or 3 shallots, sliced**

8 **ounces button or crimini mushrooms, halved or quartered**

1 **can (14½ ounces) diced tomatoes, undrained**

2 **tablespoons all-purpose flour**

½ **teaspoon dried thyme leaves**

Cheese Puff Topping (recipe follows)

Melt butter in large skillet over medium heat. Add chicken and onion. Cook and stir 3 minutes. Add mushrooms. Cook and stir 5 minutes. Add tomatoes, flour, and thyme. Cook and stir until thickened and bubbly. Cover and keep warm on low heat.

Prepare **Cheese Puff Topping**. Pour warm **Filling** into 2-quart casserole dish sprayed with non-stick cooking spray. Spoon Topping into 4 mounds on top of Filling. Bake at 400°F for 35 to 45 minutes, or until pastry is puffed and browned and filling is bubbly.

CHEESE PUFF TOPPING
YIELD: ABOUT 2 CUPS

½ **cup water**

¼ **cup (½ stick) butter or margarine, cut up**

¼ **teaspoon salt**

½ **cup all-purpose flour**

2 **eggs**

2 **ounces sharp Cheddar cheese, diced**

Heat water, butter, and salt in small saucepan over high heat to a full rolling boil. Reduce heat and quickly stir in flour, mixing vigorously until mixture leaves sides of pan in a ball.

Place flour mixture in mixer bowl. Attach bowl and flat beater to mixer. Turn to Speed 2 and add eggs, one at a time, mixing about 30 seconds after each addition. Stop and scrape bowl. Turn to Speed 4 and beat about 15 seconds. Add cheese. Turn to Stir Speed and mix about 10 seconds.

PER SERVING: ABOUT 507 CAL, 39 g PRO, 24 g CARB, 28 g FAT, 240 mg CHOL, 706 mg SOD.

CHINESE NOODLES

YIELD: 8 SERVINGS

½ **cup peanut oil**
2 **tablespoons rice vinegar or white wine vinegar**
1 **tablespoon dry sherry**
2½ **tablespoons sesame oil**
3 **tablespoons soy sauce**
1 **tablespoon crushed red pepper**

½ **teaspoon ground ginger**
1 **tablespoon brown sugar**
1 **tablespoon chopped onion**
¼ **cup diced green pepper**
1 **recipe Basic Egg Noodle Pasta (page 72) or 1½ pounds spaghetti, cooked and drained**

Combine all ingredients. Toss well and refrigerate 2 hours, stirring occasionally.

PER SERVING: ABOUT 390 CAL, 8 g PRO, 42 g CARB, 21 g FAT, 94 mg CHOL, 420 mg SOD.

HORSERADISH SAUCE

YIELD: 2 CUPS

1 **cup heavy cream**
3 **tablespoons horseradish**

¼ **teaspoon salt**
¼ **cup chopped parsley**

Place cream in mixer bowl. Attach bowl and wire whip to mixer. Turn to Speed 8 and whip until stiff peaks form. Reduce to Speed 2 and add horseradish, salt, and parsley, mixing just until combined. Serve immediately.

PER SERVING: (2 TABLESPOONS) ABOUT 27 CAL, 0 g PRO, 0 g CARB, 3 g FAT, 10 mg CHOL, 26 mg SOD.

CHINESE NOODLES

SPINACH PASTA POMODORO

YIELD: 3 CUPS

5 large tomatoes, cut into sixths	**1** teaspoon salt
3 tablespoons olive oil	**¼** teaspoon pepper
3 cloves garlic, minced	**Parmesan cheese**
½ cup chopped fresh basil	**1** recipe Spinach Pasta (see below) or 1½ pounds of spinach flat noodles, cooked and drained
1 teaspoon sugar	

Assemble Fruit/Vegetable Strainer and attach to mixer. Turn to Speed 4 and strain tomatoes. Measure out 3 cups puree and set aside.

Heat oil in a 2-quart saucepan over medium heat. Add garlic and sauté 2 minutes. Add tomato puree, basil, sugar, salt, and pepper. Reduce heat; cover and simmer for 30 minutes. Serve immediately over hot pasta with Parmesan cheese.

PER SERVING: ABOUT 364 CAL, 12 g PRO, 55 g CARB, 11 g FAT, 125 mg CHOL, 436 mg SOD.

SPINACH PASTA

YIELD: 1½ POUNDS DOUGH

1 package (10 ounces) frozen, chopped spinach, thawed	**4** large eggs (⅞ cup eggs)
1 tablespoon water	**4** cups sifted all-purpose flour

Place spinach in a towel and wring out all water until spinach feels very dry. Assemble Food Grinder using fine grinding plate and attach to mixer. Turn to Speed 4 and grind spinach. Discard unground spinach that remains in grinder body.

Place ground spinach, water, and eggs in mixer bowl. Attach bowl and flat beater to mixer. Turn to Speed 4 and mix 30 seconds. Add flour to bowl. Turn to Speed 2 and mix 45 seconds.

Remove flat beater and attach dough hook. Turn to Speed 2 and knead 1 minute.

SPINACH PASTA POMODORO

Hand knead dough for 30 seconds to 1 minute. Cover with dry towel and let rest 15 minutes before extruding through Pasta Maker.

Follow cooking instructions "To Cook Pasta," page 72.

NOTE: For best results use only Flat Noodle (Plate 3), Macaroni (Plate 4), and Lasagna (Plate 5) plates with this recipe.

PER SERVING: ABOUT 91 CAL, 3 g PRO, 16 g CARB, 1 g FAT, 0 mg CHOL, 28 mg SOD.

BASIC EGG NOODLE PASTA

YIELD: 1 ¼ POUNDS DOUGH

4 large eggs (⁷⁄₈ cup eggs)	**3½ cups sifted all-purpose flour**
1 tablespoon water	

Place eggs, water, and flour in mixer bowl. Attach bowl and flat beater to mixer. Turn to Speed 2 and mix for 30 seconds.

Remove flat beater and attach dough hook. Turn to Speed 2 and knead 2 minutes.

Hand knead dough for 30 seconds to 1 minute. Cover with dry towel and let rest 15 minutes before extruding through Pasta Maker.

PER SERVING: ABOUT 94 CAL, 4 g PRO, 17 g CARB, 1 g FAT, 42 mg CHOL, 14 mg SOD.

TIP: ***To Cook Pasta,*** Add 1 tablespoon salt and 1 tablespoon oil to 6 quarts boiling water. Gradually add pasta and continue to cook at a slow boil until pasta is "al dente" or slightly firm to the bite. Pasta floats on top of the water as it cooks, so stir occasionally to keep pasta cooking evenly. When done cooking, drain in a colander.

For Spaghetti, Flat Noodles, and Macaroni, cook entire recipe as stated above. For Lasagna, cook half the recipe at a time.

WHOLE WHEAT PASTA

YIELD: 1 ¼ POUNDS DOUGH

4 large eggs (⅞ cup eggs)	**3½ cups sifted whole wheat flour**
2 tablespoons water	

Place eggs, water, and flour in mixer bowl. Attach bowl and flat beater to mixer. Turn to Speed 2 and mix for 30 seconds.

Remove flat beater and attach dough hook. Turn to Speed 2 and knead 1 minute.

Hand knead dough for 30 seconds to 1 minute. Cover with dry towel and let rest 15 minutes before extruding through Pasta Maker.

Follow cooking instructions "To Cook Pasta," page 86.

TIP: Always sift flour directly into measuring cup before adding to bowl.

NOTE: High humidity can cause pasta dough to become sticky and difficult to extrude. To avoid this problem, prepare dough using only the sifted flour and eggs. Stop and check consistency. If dough is too dry, add the water, a teaspoon at a time, and remix using flat beater; or knead dough with wet hands.

PER SERVING: ABOUT 86 CAL, 4 g PRO, 15 g CARB, 1 g FAT, 43 mg CHOL, 14 mg SOD.

PESTO SAUCE

YIELD: 2 CUPS

2 cups fresh basil leaves	**½ teaspoon pepper**
1 cup parsley sprigs	**1 cup Parmesan cheese**
8 cloves garlic	**⅔ cup olive oil**
1 teaspoon salt	

Assemble Food Grinder using fine grinding plate and attach to mixer. Turn to Speed 4 and grind basil leaves, parsley sprigs, and garlic into mixer bowl. Add salt, pepper, and Parmesan cheese. Attach bowl and wire whip. Turn to Speed 6 and whip 1 minute. Stop and scrape bowl. Turn to Speed 8 and gradually add olive oil in a thin, steady stream, whipping until absorbed. Use about 2 tablespoons of Pesto Sauce per serving of pasta.

TIP: If Pesto Sauce is not used at once, place it in a jar and cover with a thin layer of olive oil to keep it from darkening. Refrigerate for a week or freeze for longer storage.

PER SERVING: (2 TABLESPOONS) ABOUT 63 CAL, 5 g PRO, 2 g CARB, 4 g FAT, 9 mg CHOL, 449 mg SOD.

MUSHROOM SWISS ONION QUICHE

YIELD: ONE 9-INCH PIE

½ **pound Swiss cheese**
1 **small onion, halved**
¼ **pound fresh mushrooms**
   (9-inch) Baked Pastry Shell
   (see page 131)
4 **eggs**

1 **cup heavy cream**
1 **teaspoon salt**
2 **tablespoons parsley**
   Dash hot pepper sauce
3 **slices bacon, crisply cooked**
   and crumbled

Assemble Rotor Slicer/Shredder using fine shredder cone (No. 1) and attach to mixer. Turn to Speed 4 and shred cheese and onion, keeping each separate. Exchange fine shredder cone for thick slicer cone (No. 3). Turn to Speed 4 and slice mushrooms.

Place half of shredded cheese in Baked Pastry Shell. Arrange sliced mushrooms on top of cheese. Arrange onion on top of mushrooms.

Place eggs in mixer bowl. Attach bowl and flat beater to mixer. Turn to Speed 4 and beat 3 minutes. Add cream, salt, parsley, and hot pepper sauce. Turn to Speed 4 and beat 1 minute. Pour mixture into shell.

Top with remaining cheese and sprinkle with bacon. Bake at 350°F for 30 minutes. Knife inserted in center will come out clean when done. Serve immediately.

PER SERVING: (⅛ QUICHE) ABOUT 387 CAL, 14 g PRO, 15 g CARB, 30 g FAT, 175 mg CHOL, 569 mg SOD.

SHRIMP GUMBO

YIELD: 6 SERVINGS

1 medium onion, halved	1 teaspoon sugar
1 large green pepper, seeded and quartered	½ teaspoon salt
3 stalks celery	1 bay leaf
4 tablespoons olive oil	1 teaspoon thyme
2 cloves garlic, minced	1 tablespoon chopped parsley
1 can (28 ounces) whole tomatoes, coarsely chopped	1 teaspoon hot pepper sauce
2 cans (8 ounces) tomato sauce	2 pounds medium shrimp, shelled and deveined
	Hot cooked rice

Assemble Rotor Slicer/Shredder using thick slicer cone (No. 3) and attach to mixer. Turn to Speed 4 and slice onion, green pepper, and celery, keeping each separate.

Heat oil in a 5-quart pot over medium heat. Add garlic and saute 1 minute. Add onion and saute 2 minutes. Add green pepper and celery and saute 2 minutes more.

Add tomatoes, tomato sauce, sugar, salt, bay leaf, thyme, parsley, and hot pepper sauce. Reduce heat and simmer 15 minutes. Add shrimp, stir gently and cook 4 to 5 minutes longer. Serve immediately over hot rice.

PER SERVING: ABOUT 306 CAL, 33 g PRO, 17 g CARB, 12 g FAT, 230 mg CHOL, 1006 mg SOD.

PORK CHOPS WITH SWEET POTATOES AND APPLES

YIELD: 4 SERVINGS

3 **medium sweet potatoes, peeled**
3 **medium apples, peeled and cored**
1 **small onion**
4 **slices bacon**
4 **loin chops (1 inch thick), fat trimmed**

1 **tablespoon lemon juice**
¼ **teaspoon salt**
⅛ **teaspoon pepper**
⅛ **teaspoon nutmeg**
¼ **teaspoon chervil**
1 **tablespoon chopped parsley**

Assemble Rotor Slicer/Shredder using coarse shredder cone (No. 2) and attach to mixer. Turn to Speed 4 and shred sweet potatoes, apples, and onion.

Cook bacon in 12-inch skillet over medium-high heat until crisp. Drain all but 1 tablespoon fat. Crumble bacon and set aside.

Rub pork chops with lemon juice; brown in bacon fat. Remove from pan and set aside. Drain all but 1 tablespoon fat. Add sweet potatoes, apples, and onion to pan. Cook 5 minutes, stirring occasionally. Add salt, pepper, nutmeg, and chervil; mix well.

Place vegetable mixture in a greased 9×9×2-inch pan. Arrange pork chops on top of mixture and sprinkle with chopped parsley and bacon. Cover tightly and bake at 350°F for 50 to 60 minutes, or until pork chops are tender. Serve immediately.

PER SERVING: ABOUT 307 CAL, 24 g PRO, 35 g CARB, 8 g FAT, 66 mg CHOL, 354 mg SOD.

Classic CAKES

These recipes for cakes and frostings are *impressive* enough for company but easy enough for family night

CAPPUCCINO FUDGE CUPCAKES
(page 80)

CAPPUCCINO FUDGE CUPCAKES

Pictured on page 79　　　　　　　　　　**YIELD:** 8 CUPCAKES

½ cup (1 stick) butter or margarine, softened	1¾ cups all-purpose flour
1½ cups sugar	1½ teaspoons baking powder
3 eggs	¼ teaspoon salt
¾ cup milk	Coffee Cream (recipe follows)
1 tablespoon plus 2 teaspoons instant espresso or coffee granules	Fudge Sauce (recipe follows)

Place butter in mixer bowl. Attach bowl and flat beater to mixer. Turn to Speed 6 and gradually add sugar, beating about 3 minutes, or until light and fluffy. Turn to Speed 4 and add eggs, one at a time, beating for 30 seconds after each addition. Stop and scrape bowl. Dissolve instant espresso in milk. Set aside.

Combine flour, baking powder, and salt. Turn to Stir Speed and add a third of the flour mixture alternately with half of the milk mixture, mixing 15 seconds after each addition.

Spoon batter into 8 greased and floured custard cups. Place cups on baking sheet. Bake at 350°F for 30 to 35 minutes, or until toothpick inserted into cupcake comes out clean. Remove from custard cups and cool on wire rack. Top with **Coffee Cream** and serve with **Fudge Sauce**.

COFFEE CREAM
YIELD: ABOUT 2½ CUPS

1½ cups heavy cream	1½ teaspoons instant espresso or coffee granules
¼ cup sugar	

Combine cream, sugar, and espresso in mixer bowl. Attach bowl and wire whip to mixer. Turn to Speed 8 and whip cream until stiff.

FUDGE SAUCE

4 squares (1 ounce each) semi-sweet chocolate

½ cup whipping cream
½ teaspoon ground cinnamon

Place chocolate, cream, and cinnamon in small saucepan. Cook and stir over low heat until chocolate is melted and mixture is combined.

PER SERVING: ABOUT 690 CAL, 8 g PRO, 76 g CARB, 40 g FAT, 187 mg CHOL, 291 mg SOD.

APPLESAUCE CAKE

YIELD: 1 CAKE

1½ cups all-purpose flour
1 cup whole wheat flour
1½ cups sugar
1 teaspoon baking powder
1 teaspoon baking soda
½ teaspoon salt
1½ teaspoons ground cinnamon

½ teaspoon ground nutmeg
1½ cups applesauce
½ cup (1 stick) butter or margarine, melted
2 eggs
1 cup chopped, peeled apple
½ cup chopped walnuts
Caramel Crème Frosting, if desired (page 94)

Combine dry ingredients in mixer bowl. Add applesauce, margarine, and eggs. Attach bowl and flat beater to mixer. Turn to Speed 2 and mix about 1 minute. Stop and scrape bowl. Turn to Speed 4 and beat about 30 seconds. Turn to Stir Speed and add apple and walnuts, mixing just until blended.

Pour batter into greased and floured 13×9×2-inch baking pan. Bake at 350°F for 35 to 40 minutes, or until toothpick inserted in center comes out clean. Cool completely on wire rack. Frost with **Caramel Crème Frosting**, if desired.

PER SERVING: (¹⁄₁₆ CAKE) ABOUT 318 CAL, 5 g PRO, 51 g CARB, 11 g FAT, 36 mg CHOL, 315 mg SOD.

FLUFFY FROSTING

1½ **cups sugar**	1½ **tablespoons light corn syrup**
½ **teaspoon cream of tartar**	½ **teaspoon salt**
½ **cup water**	2 **egg whites**
	1½ **teaspoons vanilla**

Place sugar, cream of tartar, salt, water, and corn syrup in a saucepan. Cook and stir over medium heat until sugar is completely dissolved, forming a syrup.

Place egg whites in mixer bowl. Attach bowl and wire whip to mixer. Turn to Speed 10 and whip until about 45 seconds, or until egg whites begin to hold shape. Continuing on Speed 10, slowly pour hot syrup into egg whites in a fine stream and whip about 5 minutes longer, or until frosting loses its gloss and stands in stiff peaks. Frost cake immediately.

PER SERVING: ABOUT 109 CAL, 1 g PRO, 27 g CARB, 0 g FAT, 0 mg CHOL, 101 mg SOD.

Frosting for 2-layer or 13×9×2-inch cake.

FLUFFY CHOCOLATE FROSTING: Melt 3 squares (1 ounce each) unsweetened chocolate with water, corn syrup, sugar, cream of tartar, and salt. Proceed as directed above.

FLUFFY PEPPERMINT FROSTING: Omit vanilla and add 1 teaspoon peppermint extract and ¼ cup crushed peppermint candy. Proceed as directed above.

FLUFFY AMARETTO FROSTING: Omit vanilla and add 2½ teaspoons Amaretto liqueur. Proceed as directed above.

FLUFFY LEMON FROSTING: Omit vanilla and add 1 teaspoon lemon extract and 2 teaspoons grated lemon peel. Proceed as directed above.

CARAMEL WALNUT BANANA TORTE

YIELD: 1 TORTE

1 **cup firmly packed brown sugar**	1 **teaspoon vanilla**
1 **cup butter (2 sticks) or margarine, softened, divided**	3 **eggs**
	2½ **cups all-purpose flour**
½ **cup whipping cream**	1¼ **teaspoons baking powder**
1 **cup chopped walnuts**	1 **teaspoon baking soda**
1½ **cups granulated sugar**	½ **teaspoon salt**
1 **cup mashed ripe banana (about 2 medium bananas)**	¾ **cup buttermilk**
	Banana Filling (recipe follows)
	½ **cup whipping cream, whipped**

Place brown sugar, ½ cup butter, and cream in small saucepan. Cook over low heat, stirring constantly, until butter melts. Divide among three 8- to 9-inch round cake pans, turning to evenly coat bottom. Divide walnuts among pans then set pans aside.

Place granulated sugar and remaining ½ cup butter in mixer bowl. Attach bowl and flat beater to mixer. Turn to Speed 2 and mix about 30 seconds. Stop and scrape bowl. Add mashed bananas and vanilla. Continuing on Speed 2, mix about 30 seconds. Continuing on Speed 2, add eggs, one at a time, mixing about 15 seconds after each addition. Stop and scrape bowl.

Combine flour, baking powder, baking soda, and salt in medium bowl. Add half of flour mixture to sugar mixture in mixer bowl. Turn to Speed 2 and mix about 30 seconds. Add buttermilk and remaining flour mixture. Gradually turn to Speed 6 and beat 30 seconds. Spread batter evenly over Topping in pans. Bake at 350°F for 25 to 30 minutes, or until toothpick inserted in centers comes out clean. Cool in pans about 3 minutes. Invert onto wire racks and completely.

Place 1 cake layer, walnut side up, on large plate. Spread with half of Filling. Arrange half of banana slices over **Banana Filling**. Top with second layer, walnut side up. Spread with remaining Filling and banana slices. Top with remaining cake layer, walnut side up. Top Torte with whipped cream. Store in refrigerator.

BANANA FILLING

- ½ **cup granulated sugar**
- 3 **tablespoons all-purpose flour**
- ¼ **teaspoon salt**
- 1 **cup low-fat milk**
- 1 **egg, beaten**

- 1 **teaspoon vanilla**
- 1 **tablespoon butter or margarine**
- 2 **medium bananas, thinly sliced, divided**

Combine sugar, flour, and salt in medium saucepan. Gradually stir in milk. Bring to boil over medium heat, stirring constantly. Stir about ¼ cup hot mixture into beaten egg in separate bowl. Pour egg mixture into saucepan. Cook until mixture is bubbly, stirring constantly. Remove from heat. Stir in vanilla and butter. Cool slightly. Refrigerate 1 hour while cake cools.

PER SERVING: (¹⁄₂₀ **TORTE) ABOUT 451 CAL, 7 g PRO, 65 g CARB, 19 g FAT, 58 mg CHOL, 384 mg SOD.**

BLUEBERRY MACADAMIA NUT SWIRL COFFEE CAKE

YIELD: 1 CAKE

1¾ **cups all-purpose flour**
½ **cup whole wheat flour**
¾ **cup firmly packed brown sugar**
¾ **cup (1½ sticks) butter or margarine, chilled and cut into small pieces**
1 **teaspoon baking powder**

½ **teaspoon baking soda**
¼ **teaspoon salt**
¾ **cup buttermilk**
1 **egg**
1 **cup blueberry pie filling**
¾ **cup chopped macadamia nuts or blanched almonds**

Place all-purpose flour, whole wheat flour, brown sugar, and butter in bowl. Attach bowl and flat beater. Turn to Stir Speed and mix until butter is the size of peas, about 3 minutes. Stop and scrape bowl. Remove ½ cup flour mixture. Set aside.

Add baking powder, baking soda, and salt to flour mixture in bowl. Turn to Stir Speed and mix 30 seconds. Add buttermilk and egg. Continuing on Stir Speed, mix just until moistened, about 30 seconds. Do not overbeat.

Spoon batter into greased 13×9×2-inch baking pan. Drop blueberry filling by tablespoonfuls on top of batter; swirl into batter. Sprinkle top with nuts and reserved flour mixture. Bake at 350°F for 30 to 40 minutes or until light golden brown.

SERVING SIZE: (¹⁄₁₆ **CAKE) ABOUT 242 CAL, 3 g PRO, 29 g CARB, 13 g FAT, 37 mg CHOL, 198 mg SOD.**

OLD-FASHIONED POUND CAKE

YIELD: 1 CAKE

3 cups all-purpose flour	**½ cup low-fat milk**
2 cups sugar	**1 teaspoon vanilla**
3 teaspoons baking powder	**1 teaspoon almond extract**
½ teaspoon salt	**6 eggs**
2 cups (4 sticks) butter, softened	

Combine dry ingredients in mixer bowl. Add butter, milk, vanilla, and almond extract. Attach bowl and flat beater to mixer. Turn to Stir Speed and mix about 1 minute. Stop and scrape bowl. Turn to Speed 6 and beat about 2 minutes. Stop and scrape bowl. Turn to Speed 2 and add eggs, one at a time, mixing about 15 seconds after each addition. Turn to Speed 4 and beat about 30 seconds.

Pour batter into greased and floured 10-inch tube pan. Bake at 350°F for 1 hour 15 minutes, or until toothpick inserted in center comes out clean. Cool completely in pan on wire rack. Remove cake from pan.

PER SERVING: (¹⁄₁₆ **CAKE) ABOUT 419 CAL, 5 g PRO, 44 g CARB, 25 g FAT, 143 mg CHOL, 378 mg SOD.**

QUICK YELLOW CAKE

YIELD: 1 CAKE

2¼ **cups all-purpose flour**	½ **cup shortening**
1⅓ **cups sugar**	1 **cup low-fat milk**
3 **teaspoons baking powder**	1 **teaspoon vanilla**
½ **teaspoon salt**	2 **eggs**

Combine dry ingredients in mixer bowl. Add shortening, milk, and vanilla. Attach bowl and flat beater to mixer. Turn to Speed 2 and mix about 1 minute. Stop and scrape bowl. Add eggs. Continuing on Speed 2, mix about 30 seconds. Stop and scrape bowl. Turn to Speed 6 and beat about 1 minute.

Pour batter into two greased and floured 8- or 9-inch round baking pans. Bake at 350°F for 30 to 35 minutes, or until toothpick inserted in center comes out clean. Cool 10 minutes. Remove from pans. Cool completely on wire rack. Frost if desired.

PER SERVING: (¹⁄₁₆ **CAKE) ABOUT 272 CAL, 4 g PRO, 42 g CARB, 10 g FAT, 37 mg CHOL, 175 mg SOD.**

BUTTERCREAM FROSTING

YIELD: 12 TO 16 SERVINGS*

¾ **cup (1½ sticks) butter or margarine, softened**	2 **cups powdered sugar**
	1½ **teaspoons vanilla**

Place butter in mixer bowl. Attach bowl and flat beater to mixer. Turn to Speed 6 and beat 30 seconds. Stop and scrape bowl.

Sift powdered sugar into bowl. Add vanilla. Turn to Speed 2 and beat 30 seconds. Stop and scrape bowl. Turn to Speed 6 and beat 2 minutes, or until fluffy.

PER SERVING: **ABOUT 181 CAL, 0 g PRO, 20 g CARB, 12 g FAT, 31 mg CHOL, 82 mg SOD.**

Frosting for 2-layer or 13×9×2-inch cake.

QUICK YELLOW CAKE

CHOCOLATE ROLL

4	**eggs, separated**	¼	**teaspoon salt**
¾	**cup sugar, divided**	¼	**cup cocoa**
½	**teaspoon vanilla**		**Whipped Cream Filling**
¾	**cup cake flour**		**(recipe follows)**
1	**teaspoon baking powder**		

Place egg yolks in mixer bowl. Attach bowl and wire whip to mixer. Turn to Speed 8 and whip until light and lemon colored, about 2 minutes. Continuing on Speed 8, gradually sprinkle in ¼ cup sugar and vanilla and beat 2 minutes more. Remove from bowl and set aside.

Place egg whites in clean mixer bowl. Attach bowl and wire whip to mixer. Turn to Speed 8 and whip until whites begin to hold shape. Continuing on Speed 8, gradually sprinkle in remaining sugar, whipping until stiff but not dry.

Fold egg yolk mixture into egg whites. Sift flour, baking powder, salt, and cocoa together. Fold into egg mixture.

Line a 10½×15½×1-inch jelly roll pan with waxed paper and grease. Pour batter into pan and bake at 375°F for 10 to 12 minutes. Remove from oven and immediately turn onto a towel sprinkled with powdered sugar. Remove waxed paper, and roll cake and towel together; cool completely.

When cool, unroll cake and spread with **Whipped Cream Filling.** Reroll and sprinkle with powdered sugar.

WHIPPED CREAM FILLING

1	**cup heavy cream**	**3**	**tablespoons sugar**
½	**teaspoon vanilla**		

Place cream and vanilla in mixer bowl. Attach bowl and wire whip to mixer. Turn to Speed 8 and whip until cream begins to thicken. Continuing on Speed 8, gradually sprinkle in sugar, whipping until stiff.

PER SERVING: (¹⁄₁₀ **CAKE) ABOUT 218 CALORIES, 4 g PRO, 27 g CARB, 11 g FAT, 118 mg CHOL, 142 mg SOD.**

CARAMEL CRÈME FROSTING

YIELD: 12 TO 16 SERVINGS*

½ **cup (1 stick) butter or margarine**

1 **cup firmly packed brown sugar**

¼ **cup low-fat milk**

1 **cup miniature marshmallows**

2 **cups powdered sugar**

½ **teaspoon vanilla**

Melt butter in medium saucepan. Add brown sugar and milk, stirring to blend. Heat to boiling. Cook about 1 minute, stirring constantly. Remove from heat. Add marshmallows. Stir until marshmallows melt and mixture is smooth.

Place powdered sugar in mixer bowl. Add brown sugar mixture and vanilla. Attach bowl and flat beater to mixer. Turn to Stir Speed and mix about 30 seconds. Turn to Speed 4 and beat about 1 minute, or until smooth and creamy. Spread on cake while warm; frosting sets as it cools.

PER SERVING: ABOUT 228 CAL, 0 g PRO, 41 g CARB, 7 g FAT, 0 mg CHOL, 98 mg SOD.

Frosting for 2-layer or 13×9×2-inch cake..

CHOCOLATE FROSTING

YIELD: 12 TO 16 SERVINGS*

1 **cup (2 sticks) butter, softened**
2 **tablespoons light corn syrup**
4 **cups powdered sugar**

2 **squares (1 ounce each) unsweetened chocolate, melted**

Place butter in mixer bowl. Attach bowl and flat beater to mixer. Turn to Speed 4 and beat about 1½ minutes, or until creamy. Stop and scrape bowl. Add corn syrup. Turn to Speed 2 and mix well. Stop and scrape bowl.

Turn to Stir Speed. Gradually add powdered sugar, mixing until blended. Turn to Speed 4 and beat about 1 minute. Stop and scrape bowl. Turn to Speed 2. Slowly add melted chocolate and mix about 1½ minutes. Stop and scrape bowl. Turn to Speed 4 and beat about 1 minute.

PER SERVING: ABOUT 325 CAL, 1 g PRO, 44 g CARB, 18 g FAT, 41 mg CHOL, 160 mg SOD.

Frosting for 2-layer or 13×9×2-inch cake

CARROT CAKE

4 eggs	**¼ teaspoon salt**
1 cup (2 sticks) butter or margarine, melted	**1 teaspoon cinnamon**
2 cups all-purpose flour	**2½ cups finely grated carrots**
1½ cups sugar	**½ cups chopped walnuts**
1½ teaspoons baking powder	**Cream Cheese Frosting (recipe follows)**

Place eggs and butter in mixer bowl. Attach bowl and flat beater to mixer. Turn to Speed 6 and beat 1 minute. Stop and scrape bowl. Add flour, sugar, baking powder, salt, and cinnamon. Turn to Speed 2 and beat 30 seconds, until combine. Reduce to Stir Speed and quickly fold in carrots and walnuts, about 10 seconds.

Pour batter into a greased and floured 9-inch springform pan. Bake at 350°F for 1 hour 15 minutes. Cake is very moist and should not be tested for doneness with an inserted toothpick. Remove cake from oven at end of baking period. Cool in pan 10 minutes, then remove and cool on wire rack. When cool, slice cake in half to form two layers. Frost with **Cream Cheese Frosting.**

CREAM CHEESE FROSTING
YIELD: 3 CUPS

4 packages (3 ounces each) cream cheese, softened	**2 teaspoons vanilla**
½ cup (1 stick) butter or margarine, softened	**2½ cups powdered sugar**

Place cream cheese, butter, and vanilla in mixer bowl. Attach bowl and flat beater to mixer. Turn to Speed 6 and beat 2 minutes. Stop and scrape bowl.

Sift powdered sugar into bowl. Turn to Speed 2 and beat 30 seconds, just until combine. Stop and scrape bowl. Turn to Speed 6 and beat 2 minutes. Refrigerate until ready to use.

PER SERVING: (¹⁄₁₆ **CAKE) ABOUT 479 CAL, 6 g PRO, 52 g CARB, 29 g FAT, 122 mg CHOL, 298 mg SOD.**

SUNSHINE CHIFFON CAKE

2 cups all-purpose flour	**1 teaspoon vanilla**
1½ cups sugar	**2 teaspoons grated lemon peel**
1 tablespoon baking powder	
½ teaspoon salt	**7 egg whites**
¾ cup cold water	**½ teaspoon cream of tartar**
½ cup vegetable oil	**Lemon Glaze (recipe follows)**
7 egg yolks, beaten	

Combine flour, sugar, baking powder, and salt in mixer bowl. Attach bowl and wire whip to mixer. Add water, vegetable oil, egg yolks, vanilla, and lemon peel. Turn to Speed 4 and beat about 1 minute. Stop and scrape bowl. Continuing on Speed 4, beat about 15 seconds. Pour mixture into another bowl. Clean mixer bowl and wire whip.

Place egg whites and cream of tartar in mixer bowl. Attach bowl and wire whip to mixer. Turn to Speed 8 and whip 2 to 2½ minutes, or until whites are stiff but not dry.

Remove bowl from mixer. Gradually fold flour mixture into egg whites with spatula, just until blended.

Pour batter into ungreased 10-inch tube pan. Bake at 325°F for 60 to 75 minutes,or until top springs back when lightly touched. Immediately invert cake onto funnel or soft drink bottle. Cool completely. Remove from pan. Drizzle with *Lemon Glaze.*

LEMON GLAZE

1 cup powdered sugar	**2 to 3 tablespoons lemon juice**
1 tablespoon butter or margarine, softened	

Combine powdered sugar and butter in small bowl. Stir in lemon juice, 1 tablespoon at a time, until glaze is of desired consistency.

PER SERVING: (¹/₁₆ **CAKE) ABOUT 256 CAL, 4 g PRO, 38 g CARB, 10 g FAT, 93 mg CHOL, 152 mg SOD.**

EASY WHITE CAKE

YIELD: 1 CAKE

2 cups all-purpose flour	**½** cup shortening
1½ cups sugar	**1** cup low-fat milk
3 teaspoons baking powder	**1** teaspoon vanilla
½ teaspoon salt	**4** egg whites

Combine dry ingredients in mixer bowl. Add shortening, milk, and vanilla. Attach bowl and flat beater to mixer. Turn to Speed 2 and mix about 1 minute. Stop and scrape bowl. Add egg whites. Turn to Speed 6 and beat about 1 minute, or until smooth and fluffy.

Pour batter into two greased and floured 8- or 9-inch round baking pans. Bake at 350°F for 30 to 35 minutes, or until toothpick inserted in center comes out clean. Cool 10 minutes. Remove from pans. Cool completely on wire rack. Frost if desired.

PER SERVING: (¹⁄₁₆ **CAKE) ABOUT 267 CAL, 4 g PRO, 42 g CARB, 9 g FAT, 2 mg CHOL, 183 mg SOD.**

ORANGE CREAM CHEESE FROSTING

YIELD: 12 TO 16 SERVINGS*

4 cups powdered sugar	**1** teaspoon orange juice
1 package (8 ounces) light cream cheese	**½** teaspoon grated orange peel

Place all ingredients in mixer bowl. Attach bowl and flat beater to mixer. Turn to Stir Speed and mix about 30 seconds, or until blended. Turn to Speed 4 and beat about 2 minutes, or until smooth and creamy.

PER SERVING: **ABOUT 196 CAL, 2 g PRO, 41 g CARB, 3 g FAT, 7 mg CHOL, 107 mg SOD.**

Frosting for 2-layer or 13×9×2-inch cake.

SOUR CREAM BUNDT CAKE

3 **cups all-purpose flour**	1 **cup (2 sticks) butter or**
½ **teaspoon salt**	**margarine, softened**
3 **teaspoons baking powder**	1 **cup sour cream**
1 **teaspoon baking soda**	1 **teaspoon vanilla**
1½ **cups sugar**	3 **eggs**
1 **teaspoon cinnamon**	1 **cup chopped nuts**

Sift flour, salt, baking powder, soda, sugar, and cinnamon into mixer bowl. Add butter, sour cream, and vanilla. Attach bowl and flat beater to mixer. Turn to Stir Speed and mix until ingredients are combined, about 30 seconds. Stop and scrape bowl. Turn to Speed 4 and beat for 1½ minutes. Stop and scrape bowl.

Turn to Stir Speed and add eggs, one at a time, beating 15 seconds after each addition. Turn to Speed 2 and beat 30 seconds. Reduce to Stir Speed and quickly add nuts, about 15 seconds.

Pour batter into greased and floured 10-inch bundt pan. Bake at 350°F for 60 to 65 minutes. Cool in pan 10 minutes, then remove and cool on wire racks.

PER SERVING: (1/16 **CAKE) ABOUT 347 CAL, 5 g PRO, 38 g CARB, 20 g FAT, 75 mg CHOL, 345 mg SOD.**

Sweet BITES

When you want just a bite

of something sweet, try

whipping up

one these cookie, bar,

or candy recipes.

CREAMY NO-COOK MINTS

(page 104)

CREAMY NO-COOK MINTS

Pictured on page 103   **YIELD:** 7 DOZEN CANDIES

1 **package (3 ounces) light cream cheese**	2 **drops green food color (or color of choice)**
¼ **teaspoon mint extract**	4¼ **to 4½ cups powdered sugar Superfine sugar**

Place cream cheese, mint extract, and food color in mixer bowl. Attach bowl and flat beater to mixer. Turn to Speed 2 and mix about 30 seconds, or until smooth. Continuing on Speed 2, gradually add powdered sugar and mix about 1½ minutes, or until mixture becomes very stiff.

To make mints, dip individual flexible candy molds into superfine sugar. Press in mint mixture. Turn out onto waxed paper covered with superfine sugar. Repeat until all mixture is used, Or: Shape mixture into ¾-inch balls, using 1 teaspoon for each ball. Roll in superfine sugar. Place on waxed paper covered with superfine sugar. Flatten slightly with thumb to form ¼-inch thick patties. If desired, press back of fork lightly on patties to form ridges.

Store mints, tightly covered, in refrigerator. Mints also freeze well.

PER SERVING: (2 MINTS) ABOUT 54 CAL, 0 g PRO, 13 g CARB, 0 g FAT, 1 mg CHOL, 12 mg SOD.

CHOCOLATE FUDGE

YIELD: ABOUT 5 DOZEN CANDIES

Butter
2 cups sugar
⅛ teaspoon salt
¾ cup evaporated milk
1 teaspoon light corn syrup

2 squares (1 ounce each)
2 tablespoons butter or margarine
1 teaspoon vanilla
2 cup chopped walnuts or pecans

Butter sides of heavy 2-quart saucepan. Combine sugar, salt, evaporated milk, corn syrup, and chocolate in pan. Cook and stir over medium heat until chocolate melts and sugar dissolves. Cook to soft ball stage (236°F) without stirring. Remove immediately from heat. Add butter without stirring. Cool to lukewarm (110°F). Stir in vanilla.

Pour mixture into mixer bowl. Attach bowl and flat beater to mixer. Turn to Speed 2 and mix about 8 minutes, or until fudge stiffens and loses its gloss. Quickly turn to Stir Speed and add walnuts, mixing just until blended. Spread in buttered 9×9×2-inch baking pan. Cool at room temperature. Cut into 1-inch squares when firm.

PER SERVING: **ABOUT 59 CAL, 1 g PRO, 7 g CARB, 3 g FAT, 1 mg CHOL, 12 mg SOD.**

BROWN EDGE WAFERS

YIELD: 2 DOZEN COOKIES

½ **cup (1 stick) butter or margarine, softened**	1 **teaspoon vanilla**
½ **cup sugar**	½ **teaspoon grated orange peel**
1 **egg**	1 **cup all-purpose flour**

Place butter and sugar in mixer bowl. Attach bowl and flat beater to mixer. Turn to Speed 6 and beat 15 seconds. Stop and scrape bowl.

Add egg, vanilla, and orange peel. Turn to Speed 6 and beat 30 seconds, until fluffy. Stop and scrape bowl. Turn to Speed 2 and add flour, mixing 15 seconds or just until blended.

Drop by teaspoonfuls onto greased baking sheets. Bake at 375°F for 8 to 10 minutes. Cool on wire racks.

PER SERVING: ABOUT 72 CAL, 1 g PRO, 8 g CARB, 4 g FAT, 19 mg CHOL, 30 mg SOD.

TIP: Drizzle cookies with melted chocolate when cool.

MACAROONS

YIELD: 2 DOZEN COOKIES

1 **can (8 ounces) almond paste**	½ **cup granulated sugar**
2 **egg whites**	1 **cup powdered sugar**

Place almond paste and egg whites in mixer bowl. Attach bowl and flat beater to mixer. Turn to Speed 4 and beat 1 minute. Stop and scrape bowl.

Add granulated sugar. Turn to Speed 4 and beat 30 seconds. Stop and scrape bowl. Sift powdered sugar into bowl. Turn to Speed 6 and beat 15 seconds.

Drop by teaspoonfuls 2 inches apart onto greased and floured baking sheets. Bake at 350°F for 12 to 15 minutes. Cool on wire racks

PER SERVING: ABOUT 80 CAL, 1 g PRO, 14 g CARB, 3 g FAT, 0 mg CHOL, 6 mg SOD.

BROWN EDGE WAFERS

BLONDIES

YIELD: 2 DOZEN BARS

½ cup plus 2 tablespoons butter or margarine
2 cups brown sugar
2 eggs
1½ teaspoons vanilla
2 cups all-purpose flour

1½ teaspoons baking powder
½ teaspoon salt
½ cup chopped walnuts
¼ cup semisweet chocolate chips

Place butter, brown sugar, eggs, and vanilla in mixer bowl. Attach bowl and flat beater to mixer. Turn to Speed 4 and beat 1 minute. Stop and scrape bowl.

Add flour, baking powder, and salt. Turn to Speed 2 and beat 15 seconds. Stop and scrape bowl. Turn to Stir Speed and add nuts and chocolate chips, mixing just until combined.

Press dough into a 13×9×2-inch greased and floured pan. Bake at 350°F for 25 to 25 minutes. Cool in pan, then cut into 3×1½-inch bars.

PER SERVING: ABOUT 181 CAL, 2 g PRO, 27 g CARB, 7 g FAT, 30 mg CHOL, 126 mg SOD.

MACADAMIA CHOCOLATE CHUNK COOKIES

YIELD: 4 DOZEN COOKIES

1   **cup firmly packed brown sugar**
¾   **cup granulated sugar**
1   **cup (2 sticks) margarine or butter, softened**
2   **teaspoons vanilla**
2   **eggs**
2¼ **cups all-purpose flour, divided**

½   **cup unsweetened cocoa powder**
1   **teaspoon baking powder**
½   **teaspoon salt**
1   **package (8 ounces) semi-sweet baking chocolate, cut into small chunks**
1   **jar (3½ ounces) macadamia nuts, coarsely chopped**

Place brown sugar, granulated sugar, butter, vanilla, and eggs in mixer bowl. Attach bowl and flat beater to mixer. Turn to Speed 2 and mix about 30 seconds. Stop and Scrape bowl. Turn to Speed 4 and beat about 1 minute. Stop and scrape bowl.

Add 1 cup flour, cocoa powder, baking powder, and salt. Turn to Stir Speed and mix about 30 seconds. Gradually add remaining 1½ cups flour and mix about 30 seconds longer. Turn to Speed 2 and mix about 30 seconds. Turn to Stir Speed and add chocolate chunks and nuts, mixing just until blended.

Drop by rounded teaspoonfuls onto greased baking sheets, about 2 inches apart. bake at 325°F for 12 to 13 minutes, or until edges are set. Do not overbake. Cool on baking sheets about 1 minute. Remove to wire racks and cool completely.

PER SERVING: ABOUT 125 CAL, 2 g PRO, 16 g CARB, 7 g FAT, 9 mg CHOL, 107 mg SOD.

PECAN SHORTBREAD COOKIES

YIELD: 2 DOZEN COOKIES

1	cup (2 sticks) butter		2½	cups all-purpose flour
1	teaspoon vanilla		½	cup chopped pecans
¾	cup brown sugar			

Place butter, vanilla, and brown sugar in mixer bowl. Attach bowl and flat beater to mixer. Turn to Speed 6 and beat 1 minute. Stop and scrape bowl.

Turn to Speed 2 and add flour then beat 30 seconds. Stop and scrape bowl. Turn to Stir Speed and quickly add pecans, mixing just until blended.

Shape dough into a log 1½ inches in diameter. Wrap in waxed paper and chill 20 minutes. Slice dough into ½-inch thick cookies. Place on greased baking sheets. Bake at 325°F for 18 to 20 minutes. Cool on wire racks.

Tip: Soft cookies should be stored between layers of waxed paper in an airtight container. A piece of apple or bread, changed frequently, will help keep cookies soft. Store crisp cookies in an airtight container with a loose-fitting lid. If they soften, place them in an oven at 300°F for 3 to 5 minutes before serving.

PER SERVING: **ABOUT 108 CAL, 2 g PRO, 21 g CARB, 2 g FAT, 0 mg CHOL, 3 mg SOD.**

DOUBLE-DECKER BUTTERSCOTCH BROWNIES

YIELD: 2 DOZEN BARS

¾ **cup butter**	1 **cup all-purpose flour**
2 **cups sugar**	**Butterscotch Glaze**
2 **teaspoons vanilla**	**(recipe follows)**
3 **eggs**	**Chocolate Ganache**
¾ **cup unsweetened cocoa**	**(recipe follows)**

Place butter, sugar, and vanilla in mixer bowl. Attach bowl and flat beater to mixer. Turn to Speed 2 and mix about 30 seconds. Turn to Speed 6 and beat until creamy, about 2 minutes. Stop and scrape bowl. Turn to Speed 4 and add eggs one at a time, beating about 15 seconds after each addition. Stop and scrape bowl. Add remaining brownie ingredients. Turn to Speed 2 and mix until well blended, about 30 seconds.

Pour into 15½×10½-inch jelly-roll pan that has been lined with foil and greased. Bake at 350°F for 14 to 16 minutes or until top springs back when touched lightly in the center. Remove from oven and cool in pan 2 minutes. Invert onto cutting board, remove foil, and flip right-side up onto wire rack; cool completely.

BUTTERSCOTCH GLAZE

1 **package (about 11 ounces) butterscotch-flavor baking chips**	¼ **cup water**
	¼ **cup sugar**
	1 **tablespoon light corn syrup**

Place butterscotch chips in mixer bowl. Attach bowl and flat beater to mixer. Bring water, sugar, and corn syrup to boil in small saucepan over medium high heat. Turn to mixer to Stir Speed and carefully pour in hot syrup. Mix until smooth. Cool slightly but use while warm; mixture sets as it cools.

CHOCOLATE GANACHE

½ **cup whipping cream**
1 **cup chocolate chips**

Heat cream in small saucepan over medium-low heat until bubbles appear around edge of pan. Pour over chocolate chips and stir constantly until mixture is smooth and begins to thicken. Use while warm; mixture thickens and sets as it cools.

Pour Butterscotch Glaze onto brownie and spread evenly. Before glaze sets, slice brownie layer in half and stack on half on the other. Cool until glaze sets. drizzle with Chocolate Ganache. Slice into $2 \times 1\frac{3}{4}$-inch bars once ganache sets.

PER SERVING: **ABOUT 284 CAL, 2 g PRO, 37 g CARB, 15 g FAT, 49 mg CHOL, 68 mg SOD.**

ALMOND POPPY SEED COOKIES

YIELD: 2½ DOZEN COOKIES

½ cup sugar
½ cup firmly packed brown
  sugar
½ cup (1 stick) butter or
  margarine, softened
1 egg
½ teaspoon almond extract

1⅔ cups all-purpose flour
2 tablespoons poppy seeds
1 teaspoon baking powder
¼ teaspoon salt
½ cup chopped, unblanched
  almonds

Place sugar, brown sugar, and butter in bowl. Attach bowl and flat beater to mixer. Turn to Speed 4 and beat 1 minute. Continuing on Speed 4, add egg and almond extract and beat 1 minute. Combine flour, poppy seeds, baking powder, and salt. Turn to Stir Speed and add flour mixture, beating just until combined.

Shape into 1-inch balls, roll in chopped almonds and place on greased baking sheets. Bake at 375°F for 10 to 12 minutes or until lightly browned. Cool on wire racks.

PER SERVING: ABOUT 98 CAL, 1 g PRO, 13 g CARB, 5 g FAT, 15 mg CHOL, 63 mg SOD.

FUDGE BROWNIES

YIELD: 2 DOZEN BARS

1 cup (2 sticks) margarine or butter, softened, divided	**3 eggs**
4 squares (1 ounce each) unsweetened chocolate	**1 cup all-purpose flour**
	½ teaspoon salt
2 cups sugar	**1 cup chopped walnuts or pecans**
1 teaspoon vanilla	

Melt ½ cup margarine and chocolate in small saucepan over low heat; set aside to cool.

Place remaining ½ cup margarine, sugar, and vanilla in mixer bowl. Attach bowl and flat beater to mixer. Turn to Speed 2 and mix about 30 seconds. Turn to Speed 6 and beat about 2 minutes. Turn to Speed 4. Add eggs, one at a time, beating about 15 seconds after each addition. Stop and scrape bowl.

Add cooled chocolate mixture. Turn to Speed 2 and mix about 30 seconds. Stop and scrape bowl. Add all remaining ingredients. Turn to Stir Speed and mix until well blended, about 30 seconds.

Pour into greased and floured 13×9×2-inch baking pan. Bake at 350°F for 45 minutes. Cool in pan on wire rack.

PER SERVING: ABOUT 215 CAL, 3 g PRO, 24 g CARB, 14 g FAT, 27 mg CHOL, 140 mg SOD.

CHOCOLATE CHIP COOKIES

YIELD: 4½ DOZEN COOKIES

1 **cup granulated sugar**	1 **teaspoon baking soda**
1 **cup brown sugar**	1 **teaspoon salt**
1 **cup (2 sticks) butter or**	3 **cups all-purpose flour**
margarine, softened	12 **ounces semi-sweet**
2 **eggs**	**chocolate chips**
1½ **teaspoons vanilla**	

Place sugars, butter, eggs, and vanilla in mixer bowl. Attach bowl and flat beater to mixer. Turn to Speed 2 and mix about 30 seconds. Stop and scrape bowl. Turn to Speed 4 and beat about 30 seconds. Stop and scrape bowl.

Turn to Stir Speed. Gradually add baking soda, salt, and flour to sugar mixture and mix about 2 minutes. Turn to Speed 2 and mix about 30 seconds. Stop and scrape bowl. Add chocolate chips. Turn to Stir Speed and mix about 15 seconds.

Drop rounded teaspoonfuls onto greased baking sheets, about 2 inches apart. Bake at 375°F for 10 to 12 minutes. Remove from baking sheets immediately and cool on wire racks.

PER SERVING: ABOUT 117 CAL, 1 g PRO, 17 g CARB, 5 g FAT, 8 mg CHOL, 106 mg SOD.

DIVINITY

YIELD: ABOUT 3½ DOZEN CANDIES

3 **cups sugar**
¾ **cup light corn syrup**
½ **cup water**
2 **pasteurized egg whites**

1 **teaspoon almond extract**
1 **cup chopped walnuts or
    pecans**

Place sugar, corn syrup, and water in heavy saucepan. Cook and stir over medium heat to hard ball stage (248°F). Remove from heat and let stand until temperature drops to 220°F; do not stir.

Place egg whites in mixer bowl. Attach bowl and wire whip to mixer. Turn to Speed 8 and whip until soft peaks form, about 1 minute. Gradually add syrup in a fine stream and whip about 2½ minutes longer.

Turn to Speed 4. Add almond extract and whip until mixture starts to become dry, 20 to 25 minutes. Turn to Stir Speed and add walnuts, mixing just until blended.

Drop mixture from measuring tablespoon onto waxed paper or greased baking sheet to form patties.

PER SERVING: **(2 CANDIES) ABOUT 192 CAL, 2 g PRO, 40 g CARB, 4 g FAT, 0 mg CHOL, 15 mg SOD.**

PEANUT BUTTER COOKIES

YIELD: 3 DOZEN COOKIES

½ **cup peanut butter**
½ **cup (1 stick) butter or margarine, softened**
½ **cup granulated sugar**
½ **cup brown sugar**

1 **egg**
½ **teaspoon vanilla**
½ **teaspoon baking soda**
¼ **teaspoon salt**
1¼ **cups all-purpose flour**

Place peanut butter and butter in mixer bowl. Attach bowl and flat beater to mixer. Turn to Speed 6 and beat until mixture is smooth, about 1 minute. Stop and scrape bowl. Add sugars, egg, and vanilla. Turn to Speed 4 and beat about 1 minute. Stop and scrape bowl.

Turn to Stir Speed. Gradually add all remaining ingredients to sugar mixture and mix about 30 seconds. Turn to Speed 2 and mix about 30 seconds.

Roll dough into 1-inch balls. Place about 2 inches apart on ungreased baking sheets. Press flat with fork in a criss-cross pattern to ¼-inch thickness.

Bake at 375°F until golden brown, about 10 to 12 minutes. Remove from baking sheets immediately and cool on wire racks.

PER SERVING: ABOUT 83 CAL, 2 g PRO, 10 g CARB, 4 g FAT, 6 mg CHOL, 81 mg SOD.

LEMON CREAM CHEESE BARS

YIELD: 4 DOZEN BARS

2¼ **cups plus 2 tablespoons all-purpose flour, divided**

1 **cup powdered sugar, divided**

1 **cup (2 sticks) chilled butter, cut into chunks**

1 **package (8 ounces) light cream cheese**

6 **eggs, divided**

1 **teaspoon vanilla**

2 **cups granulated sugar**

1 **teaspoon grated lemon peel**

¼ **cup lemon juice**

   Powdered sugar (optional)

Place 2 cups flour, ½ cup powdered sugar, and butter in mixer bowl. Attach bowl and flat beater to mixer. Turn to Stir Speed and mix about 1 minute, or until well blended and mixture starts to stick together. Press into ungreased 15½×10½×1-inch baking pan. Bake at 350°F for 14 to 16 minutes, or until set.

NOTE: Check Crust after 10 minutes and prick with fork if it puffs up during baking. Remove from oven.

Meanwhile, clean mixer bowl and beater. Place cream cheese, remaining ½ cup powdered sugar, 2 tablespoons flour, 2 eggs, and vanilla in mixer bowl. Attach bowl and flat beater to mixer. Turn to Stir Speed and mix about 30 seconds. Turn to Speed 4 and beat about 2 minutes, or until smooth and creamy. Pour over partially baked crust. Return to oven and bake at 350°F for another 6 to 7 minutes, or until filling is slightly set. Remove from oven.

Meanwhile, clean mixer bowl and beater. Place all remaining ingredients except lemon juice in mixer bowl. Attach bowl and flat beater to mixer. Turn to Stir Speed and mix about 20 seconds. Turn to Speed 2. Gradually add lemon juice and mix about 20 seconds, or until well blended. Pour over cream cheese filling. Return to oven and bake at 350°F for another 14 to 16 minutes, or until filling is set.

NOTE: Filling may puff up during baking but will fall when removed from oven. Sprinkle with powdered sugar, if desired. Cool completely in pan.

PER SERVING: **ABOUT 115 CAL, 2 g PRO, 16 g CARB, 5 g FAT, 39 mg CHOL, 65 mg SOD.**

RAISIN-APRICOT OATMEAL COOKIES

YIELD: 4 DOZEN COOKIES

½ **cup (1 stick) butter or margarine**
½ **cup shortening**
¾ **cup granulated sugar**
¼ **cup packed brown sugar**
2 **teaspoons vanilla**
2 **eggs**

2 **cups quick cooking oats**
1½ **cups all-purpose flour**
1 **teaspoon baking soda**
½ **teaspoon salt**
¾ **cup raisins**
½ **cup chopped dried apricots**

Place butter, shortening, sugars, vanilla, and eggs in mixer bowl. Attach bowl and flat beater to mixer. Turn to Speed 2 and mix about 30 seconds. Stop mixer and scrape bowl. Turn to Speed 4 and beat about 30 seconds. Stop and scrap bowl. Add oats, flour, baking soda, salt, raisins, and apricots. Turn to Speed 2 and mix about 30 seconds.

Drop by rounded teaspoonfuls onto greased baking sheets. Bake at 375°F for 8 to 10 minutes, or until light golden brown.

PER SERVING: ABOUT 91 CAL, 1 g PRO, 12 g CARB, 5 g FAT, 14 mg CHOL, 74 mg SOD.

Delicious DESSERTS

Truly extraordinary

desserts to finish

any meal.

CHOCOLATE PECAN PIE

(page 130)

CHOCOLATE PECAN PIE

Pictured on page 129

YIELD: ONE 9-INCH PIE

4 **eggs**	2 **cups pecan halves**
1 **cup sugar**	**(9-inch) One-Crust Pie**
1 **cup dark corn syrup**	**Pastry, unbaked (page**
3 **squares (1 ounce each)**	**131)**
unsweetened chocolate,	
melted	

Place eggs, sugar, and corn syrup in mixer bowl. Attach bowl and flat beater to mixer. Turn to Speed 6 and beat 1 minute. Stop and scrape bowl.

Turn to Speed 4 and gradually add chocolate; beat 1 minute, until well blended. Reduce to Stir Speed and quickly add pecans. Pour mixture into unbaked Pie Pastry in ungreased pie plate. Bake at 350°F for 35 to 45 minutes or until slightly soft in center.

PER SERVING: (⅛ PIE) ABOUT 757 CAL, 11 g PRO, 89 g CARB, 44 g FAT, 113 mg CHOL, 339 mg SOD.

COUNTRY PEAR PIE

YIELD: ONE 9-INCH PIE

¾ **cup brown sugar**	8-10 **medium pears (about**
3 **tablespoons all-purpose**	**2½ pounds) pared, cored**
flour	**and thinly sliced**
⅛ **teaspoon salt**	2 **tablespoons lemon juice**
Dash ground cloves	2 **tablespoons butter or**
Dash nutmeg	**margarine**
⅓ **cup heavy cream**	**(9-inch) Two-Crust Pie**
	Pastry, unbaked
	(page 131)

In a small bowl, combine brown sugar, flour, salt, cloves, and nutmeg. Stir in cream. In another bowl, sprinkle lemon juice over pears. Add brown sugar and cream mixture and mix well. Set aside.

Divide pastry in half. Roll to ⅛-inch thickness and line a 9-inch pie plate. Fill with pear mixture and dot with butter. Roll out remaining pastry and cut into ½-inch strips. Weave strips into a lattice on top of pears. Seal and crimp edges. Bake at 400°F for 35 to 40 minutes.

PER SERVING: (⅛ PIE) ABOUT 488 CAL, 5 g PRO, 70 g CARB, 22 g FAT, 29 mg CHOL, 309 mg SOD.

PIE PASTRY

2¼ cups all-purpose flour
¾ teaspoon salt
½ cup shortening, well chilled

2 tablespoons butter or margarine, well chilled
5 to 6 tablespoons cold water

Place flour and salt in mixer bowl. Attach bowl and flat beater to mixer. Turn to Stir Speed and mix about 15 seconds. Cut shortening and butter into pieces and add to flour mixture. Turn to Stir Speed and mix until shortening particles are size of small peas, 30 to 45 seconds.

Continuing on Stir Speed, add water, 1 tablespoon at a time, mixing until ingredients are moistened and dough begins to hold together. Divide dough in half. Pat each half into a smooth ball and flatten slightly. Wrap in plastic wrap. Chill in refrigerator 15 minutes.

Roll one half of dough to ⅛ inch thickness between sheets of waxed paper. Fold pastry into quarters. Ease into 8- or 9-inch pie plate and unfold, pressing firmly against bottom and sides.

For One-Crust Pie: Fold edge under. Crimp as desired. Add desired pie filling. Bake as directed.

For Two-Crust Pie: Trim pastry even with edge of pie plate. Using second half of dough, roll out another pastry crust. Add desired pie filling. Top with second pastry crust. Seal edge. Crimp as desired. Cut slits for steam to escape. Bake as directed.

For Baked Pastry Shell: Fold edge under. Crimp as desired. Prick sides and bottom with fork. Bake at 450°F for 8 to 10 minutes, or until lightly browned. Cool completely on wire rack and fill.

Alternate Method for Baked Pastry Shell: Fold edge under. Crimp as desired. Line shell with foil. Fill with pie weights or dried beans. Bake at 450°F for 10 to 12 minutes, or until edges are lightly browned. Remove pie weights and foil. Cool completely on wire rack and fill.

PER SERVING (ONE CRUST): **ABOUT 134 CAL, 2 g PRO, 13 g CARB, 8 g FAT, 0 mg CHOL, 118 mg SOD.**

PER SERVING (TWO CRUSTS): **ABOUT 267 CAL, 4 g PRO, 27 g CARB, 16 g FAT, 0 mg CHOL, 236 mg SOD.**

KEY LIME PIE

2 cups sugar, divided
¼ cup plus 2 tablespoons cornstarch
¼ teaspoon salt
½ cup fresh key lime juice
½ cup cold water
3 eggs, separated
2 tablespoons butter or margarine

½ cups boiling water
1 teaspoon grated fresh lime peel
Green food coloring (if desired)
¼ teaspoon cream of tartar
(9-inch) Baked Pastry Shell (page 131)

Combine 1½ cups sugar, cornstarch, and salt in a 2-quart saucepan. Add lime juice, water, and egg yolks; blend well. Add butter and gradually add boiling water. Bring mixture to a boil over medium heat and cook 3 minutes, stirring constantly. Stir in lime peel and green food coloring. Remove from heat and cool 20 minutes.

Place egg whites in mixer bowl. Attach bowl and wire whip to mixer. Turn to Speed 8 and whip until frothy. Add cream of tartar and whip until soft peaks form. Continuing on Speed 8, gradually add remaining sugar, beating until stiff peaks form.

Pour cooled filling into pie shell. Lightly pile meringue on filling and spread to edges. Bake at 350°F for 15 minutes, or until lightly browned. Cool completely before serving.

PER SERVING: (⅛ **PIE) ABOUT 398 CAL, 4 g PRO, 69 g CARB, 12 g FAT, 91 mg CHOL, 240 mg SOD.**

RUSTIC APPLE TART

YIELD: ONE 9-INCH TART

2½ **pounds (about 6 large) tart green apples, peeled, thinly sliced**
2 **tablespoons lemon juice**
¼ **cup granulated sugar**
⅓ **cup light brown sugar**

½ **cup flour**
½ **teaspoon cinnamon**
¼ **cup butter, softened**
(9-inch) One-Crust Pie Pastry, unbaked (page 131)

Toss together apples, lemon, and granulated sugar. Set aside

Place all remaining ingredients except Pie Pastry in mixer bowl. Attach bowl and flat beater to mixer. Turn to Speed 2 and mix until crumbly. Set aside.

Roll out pastry into a 13-inch circle. Transfer to baking sheet (it's OK if pastry hangs over edge of baking sheet).

Gently mound apples in center of pastry, leaving a 2-inch border of dough on all sides. Sprinkle apples with cinnamon sugar mixture. Fold pastry up over filling, pleating as necessary to fit snuggly around apples. Gently press dough to filling, reinforcing shape.

Bake at 400°F until pastry is golden brown and apples are tender, for about 30 minutes. Cool tart on baking sheet on wire rack 10 minutes; serve warm.

PER SERVING: (⅛ TART) ABOUT 452 CAL, 5 g PRO, 60 g CARB, 21 g FAT, 23 mg CHOL, 290 mg SOD.

VANILLA CREAM PIE

YIELD: ONE 9-INCH PIE

1 **cup sugar, divided**	1 **tablespoon margarine or**
6 **tablespoons all-purpose**	**butter**
flour	1 **teaspoon vanilla**
¼ **teaspoon plus ⅛ teaspoon**	**(9-inch) Baked Pastry Shell**
salt, divided	**(see page 131)**
2½ **cups low-fat milk**	¼ **teaspoon cream of tartar**
3 **eggs, separated**	

Combine ½ cup sugar, flour, and ¼ teaspoon salt in heavy saucepan. Add milk and cook over medium heat until thickened, stirring constantly. Reduce heat to low. Cook, covered, about 10 minutes longer, stirring occasionally. Set aside.

Place egg yolks in mixer bowl. Attach bowl and wire whip to mixer. Turn to Speed 8 and whip about 1 minute. Slowly stir small amount of milk mixture into yolks. Add yolk mixture to saucepan. Cook over medium heat 3 to 4 minutes, stirring constantly. Remove from heat. Add margarine and vanilla; cool. Pour into Baked Pastry Shell.

Place cream of tartar, remaining salt, and egg whites in mixer bowl. Attach bowl and wire whip to mixer. Gradually turn to Speed 8 and whip about 1 minute, or until soft peaks form. Turn to Speed 4. Gradually add remaining sugar and whip about 1 minute, or until stiff peaks form.

Lightly pile meringue on pie and spread to edge. Bake at 325°F for 15 minutes, or until lightly browned.

PER SERVINGS: (⅛ **PIE) ABOUT 332 CAL, 7 g PRO, 47 g CARB, 13 g FAT, 86 mg CHOL, 297 mg SOD.**

Variations

CHOCOLATE CREAM PIE

Melt 2 squares (1 ounce each) unsweetened chocolate and add to filling along with margarine and

vanilla. Proceed as directed above.

PER SERVING: (⅛ PIE) ABOUT 368 CAL, 8 g PRO, 49 g CARB, 16 g FAT, 86 mg CHOL, 298 mg SOD.

BANANA CREAM PIE

Slice 2 or 3 bananas into Baked Pastry Shell before adding filling. Proceed as directed above.

PER SERVING: (⅛ PIE) ABOUT 359 CAL, 8 g PRO, 54 g CARB, 13 g FAT, 86 mg CHOL, 298 mg SOD.

COCONUT CREAM PIE

Add ½ cup flaked coconut to filling before pouring into Baked Pastry Shell. Before baking, Sprinkle ¼ cup flaked coconut on meringue. Proceed as directed above.

PER SERVING: (⅛ PIE) ABOUT 376 CAL, 8 g PRO, 51 g CARB, 16 g FAT, 86 mg CHOL, 320 mg SOD.

WAFER TORTE

7 squares (1 ounce each) semisweet chocolate	**1** package (8 ounces) chocolate wafer cookies
6 eggs, separated	**⅓** cup Amaretto liqueur
2 teaspoons vanilla	**½** cup heavy cream
	Cocoa powder (optional)

Melt chocolate in double broiler over boiling water. Add egg yolks and vanilla; beat well. Remove from heat and set aside.

Place egg whites in mixer bowl. Attach bowl and wire whip to mixer. Turn to Speed 8 and whip until stiff but not dry. Reduce to Stir Speed and quickly add chocolate mixture, mixing just until combined.

Arrange half of wafers in the bottom of a 9-inch springform pan. Brush wafers with half of Amaretto and top with half of chocolate mixture. Repeat with remaining ingredients. Refrigerate until set, about 5 hours.

When ready to serve, unmold from pan and place on serving plate. Place cream in mixer bowl. Attach bowl and wire whip to mixer. Turn to Speed 10 and whip cream until stiff. Serve torte with dollops of whipped cream; sprinkle with cocoa, if desired.

PER SERVING: (⅛ **TORTE) ABOUT 392 CAL, 9 g PRO, 39 g CARB, 21 g FAT, 180 mg CHOL, 224 mg SOD.**

ALMOND DACQUOISE

YIELD: ONE 8-INCH CAKE

6	ounces blanched almonds, ground	¼	teaspoon cream of tartar
1	cup powdered sugar	3	tablespoons sugar
1½	tablespoons cornstarch	1¼	teaspoons vanilla
6	egg whites	¼	teaspoon almond extract
⅛	teaspoon salt		Chocolate Buttercream Filling (recipe follows)

Combine almonds, powdered sugar, and cornstarch; set aside.

Place egg whites in bowl. Attach bowl and wire whip to mixer. Turn to Speed 6 and whip until foamy. Add salt and cream of tartar and continue whipping until soft peaks form. Sprinkle in sugar, vanilla, and almond extract, beating until stiff peaks form. Reduce to Stir Speed and quickly add almond mixture, mixing just until blended.

Using a pastry bag fitted with large (½-inch) plain tip, pipe mixture onto greased and floured baking sheets to form three 8-inch circles. Bake at 250°F for 35 to 45 minutes. Remove from baking sheets and cool on aluminum foil. Fill and frost with **Chocolate Buttercream Filling**.

CHOCOLATE BUTTERCREAM FILLING

2	egg yolks	¾	cup (1½ sticks) butter or margarine, softened
1	cup powdered sugar	½	teaspoon vanilla
2	squares (1 ounce each) semisweet chocolate, melted		

Place egg yolks in bowl. Attach bowl and wire whip to mixer. Turn to Speed 6 and whip 2 minutes. Stop and scrape bowl.

Turn to Speed 4 and gradually add powdered sugar, chocolate, butter, and vanilla; continue beating until fluffy, about 5 minutes.

PER SERVING: (⅛ **CAKE) ABOUT 491 CAL, 9 g PRO, 45 g CARB, 33 g FAT, 102 mg CHOL, 272 mg SOD.**

LEMON CURD TART WITH FRESH BLUEBERRIES

YIELD: 6 SERVINGS

4 sheets phyllo dough (12×17-inches)	**Lemon Curd Filling (recipe follows)**
⅔ **cup butter, melted**	½ **pint fresh blueberries**

Place one sheet of phyllo dough on a clean work surface. Keep the remaining sheets of dough under a damp cloth until ready to use. Brush the surface of the sheet with butter. Place another sheet on top and brush with butter. Repeat with remaining dough sheets and butter.

Cut the dough into 6 equal squares. Fit one square into each cup of a well greased muffin tin. Pleat dough to fit if necessary. Work quickly so dough does not dry out. Bake at 375°F for 12 to 14 minutes.

To serve, place one-sixth of **Lemon Curd Filling** (about ⅓ cup) into each tart shell. Sprinkle each with fresh blueberries. Serve immediately.

LEMON CURD FILLING

¾ **cup sugar**	**6 large egg yolks**
½ **cup plus 1 tablespoon lemon juice**	½ **cup (1 stick) butter, at room temperature**

Place sugar and lemon juice in mixer bowl. Attach bowl and wire whip to mixer. Turn to Speed 4 and mix 1 minute.

Increase to Speed 6 and add egg yolks, one at a time, whipping about 30 seconds after each addition. Continuing on Speed 6, add butter, one tablespoon at a time, mixing about 15 seconds after each addition. Whip an additional 30 seconds. Mixture will appear curdled.

Transfer mixture to medium saucepan. Cook over medium-low heat, stirring constantly, until mixture is thick and smooth and just begins to bubble, about 7 to 8 minutes. Do not allow mixture to boil.

Pour filling into a medium bowl and press plastic wrap onto the surface of the lemon curd. Refrigerate until cold, at least 4 hours.

PER SERVING: ABOUT 544 CAL, 4 g PRO, 36 g CARB, 44 g FAT, 315 mg CHOL, 456 mg SOD.

HIDDEN PUMPKIN PIE

YIELD: 6 SERVINGS

1½ **cups canned solid-pack pumpkin**

1 **cup evaporated fat-free milk**

½ **cup cholesterol-free egg substitute**

¼ **cup no-calorie sugar substitute**

1 **teaspoon pumpkin pie spice**

1¼ **teaspoons vanilla, divided**

3 **egg whites**

¼ **teaspoon cream of tartar**

⅓ **cup honey**

Place pumpkin, evaporated milk, egg substitute, sugar substitute, pumpkin pie spice, and 1 teaspoon vanilla in mixer bowl. Attach bowl and flat beater to mixer. Turn to Speed 2 and mix 30 seconds. Stop and scrape bowl. Turn to Speed 4 and mix until smooth, about 1 minute. Divide evenly among six (6-ounce) custard cups or souffle dishes. Place in shallow baking dish or pan. Pour boiling water around custard cups or souffle dishes to depth of 1 inch. Bake 350°F for 25 minutes.

Meanwhile, place egg whites, cream of tartar, and remaining ¼ teaspoon vanilla in cleaned mixer bowl. Attach bowl and wire whip to mixer. Gradually turn to Speed 8 and whip about 1 minute, or until soft peaks form. Reduce to Speed 4 and gradually add honey, whipping until stiff peaks form, about 1 minute.

Spread egg white mixture on top of hot pumpkin mixture. Return to oven and bake 15 to 16 minutes or until tops are golden brown. Let stand 10 minutes. Serve warm.

PER SERVING: ABOUT 148 CAL, 8 g PRO, 27 g CARB, 2 g FAT, 54 mg CHOL, 133 mg SOD.

POTS DE CRÈME AU CHOCOLAT

2 cups heavy cream	**4 squares (1 ounce each) semisweet chocolate, melted**
1 tablespoon sugar	**5 egg yolks**

Heat cream and sugar in double boiler over boiling water, stirring constantly, until sugar is dissolved. Add chocolate and stir until well blended. Remove from heat and set aside.

Place egg yolks in mixer bowl. Attach bowl and wire whip to mixer. Turn to Speed 8 and whip 1 minute. Reduce to Speed 2 and gradually add cream mixture, whipping until well blended.

Fill six (6-ounce) custard cups or crème pots ⅔ full. Place cups in a 13×9×2-inch pan, and pour boiling water to fill pan 1½ inches deep. Bake at 325°F until firm, 20 to 25 minutes. Chill at least 2 hours.

PER SERVING: **ABOUT 401 CAL, 4 g PRO, 16 g CARB, 37 g FAT, 216 mg CHOL, 34 mg SOD.**

LEMON SOUFFLÉ

2	**tablespoons butter or margarine**	**3**	**tablespoons all-purpose flour**
⅓	**cup plus 3 tablespoons sugar, divided**	**¾**	**cup milk**
2	**tablespoons grated fresh lemon peel**	**⅓**	**cup fresh lemon juice**
		5	**eggs, separated**

Grease a 1½-quart soufflé dish with 2 tablespoon butter. Combine 3 tablespoons sugar and 2 tablespoon grated lemon peel. Sprinkle souffle dish with mixture; set aside.

Melt remaining butter in saucepan over medium heat. Add flour and blend well; cook 1 minute. Gradually add milk, stirring until smooth. Add sugar and bring to a boil, stirring constantly for 30 seconds. Add lemon juice and remaining lemon peel. Place mixture in bowl. Turn to Speed 4 and beat 1 minute. Stop and scrape bowl. Turn to Speed 6 and add egg yolks, one at a time, beating 15 seconds after each addition. Remove from bowl and set aside.

Place egg whites in clean bowl. Attach bowl and wire whip. Turn to Speed 8 and whip until stiff but not dry. Gently fold egg yolk mixture into egg whites. Pour into souffle dish. Run a knife around souffle dish inserted 1½ inches deep and 1 inch from the edge.

Place souffle dish in a 13×9×2-inch pan and add boiling water 1 inch in depth. Bake at 350°F for 25 to 30 minutes. Serve immediately.

PER SERVING: (⅙ SOUFFLÉ) ABOUT 193 CAL, 7 g PRO, 23 g CARB, 9 g FAT, 189 mg CHOL, 100 mg SOD.

LEMONY LIGHT CHEESECAKE

YIELD: 1 CHEESECAKE

15 **reduced-fat creme-filled chocolate sandwich cookies, finely crushed (about 1½ cups)**

2 **tablespoons butter or margarine, melted**

3 **packages (8 ounces each) light cream cheese**

1 **cup sugar**

1 **tablespoon all-purpose flour**

4 **eggs**

¼ **cup lemon juice**

1 **teaspoon lemon peel**

Combine crushed cookies and butter in medium bowl; mix well. Press mixture firmly into bottom of greased springform pan. Refrigerated until needed.

Place cream cheese, sugar, and flour in mixer bowl. Attach bowl and flat beater to mixer. Turn to Speed 2 and mix about 30 seconds. Stop and scrape bowl. Turn to Speed 2 and mix about 30 seconds longer. Stop and scrape bowl.

Add eggs, lemon juice, and lemon peel. Turn to Stir Speed and mix about 30 seconds. Stop and scrape bowl. Turn to Speed 2 and mix 15 to 30 seconds longer, just until blended. Do not overbeat. Pour into prepared crust.

Place top oven rack in center of oven. Place pan of hot water on bottom rack of oven. Place cheesecake on rack in center of oven. Bake at 325°F for 50 to 60 minutes, or until cheesecake is set when pan is jiggled slightly. Do not overbake.

Turn off oven; open oven door. Let cheesecake stand in oven 30 minutes. Remove from oven. Cool completely on wire rack away from drafts. Cover and refrigerate 6 to 8 hours before serving.

PER SERVING: (¹⁄₁₆ **CHEESECAKE) ABOUT 169 CAL, 6 g PRO, 20 g CARB, 7 g FAT, 68 mg CHOL, 214 mg SOD.**

DOUBLE CHOCOLATE MOUSSE WITH RASPBERRY SAUCE

YIELD: 6 SERVINGS*

6 **ounces bittersweet chocolate, chopped in ¾-inch chunks**
6 **ounces white chocolate, chopped in ¾-inch chunks**

2 **cups whipping cream**
Raspberry Sauce (recipe follows)

Place bittersweet chocolate in one 3- to 4-cup microwave-safe bowl. Place white chocolate in a second microwave-safe bowl. Cover each with waxed paper. Place one bowl at a time into microwave oven and heat on HIGH for 1½ minutes. Stop and stir. If chocolate is not melted, repeat process for 30 seconds at a time, or until melted. Stop and stir.

Heat Cream in a heavy saucepan over medium heat until very hot, but do not boil. Remove from heat. Pour 1 cup of cream into each of the chocolate bowls. Stir each until completely mixed. Cover bowls and refrigerate about 2 hours.

Pour white chocolate mixture into mixer bowl. Attach bowl and wire whip to mixer. Gradually turn to Speed 6 and beat 4 to 4½ minutes, or until soft peaks form. Spoon about ⅓ cup mixture into each of 6 stemmed dessert dishes. Set aside.

Pour bittersweet chocolate mixture into mixer bowl. Gradually turn to Speed 6, and beat about 3 minutes, or until soft peaks form. Spoon about ⅓ cup mixture over white chocolate layer. Cover dishes with plastic wrap or foil. Refrigerate 8 hours, or overnight.

RASPBERRY SAUCE

1 **package (14 to 16 ounces) frozen unsweetened raspberries, thawed**

¼ **cup water**
¼ **cup sugar**
1 **tablespoon cornstarch**

Place raspberries in blender container. Cover and blend until smooth. Pour mixture into wire mesh strainer over a small saucepan; press with back of spoon to squeeze out liquid. Discard seeds and pulp in strainer.

Add remaining ingredients to saucepan. Cook over medium heat, stirring constantly, until thickened and bubbly. Remove from heat and cool. Store sauce in covered container in refrigerator. Stir before using.

Spoon Raspberry Sauce over chocolate in dessert dishes before serving.

PER SERVING: ABOUT 664 CAL, 6 g PRO, 53 g CARB, 48 g FAT, 115 mg CHOL, 57 mg SOD.

²⁄₃ cup mousse and ¼ cup raspberry sauce per serving.

MANGO SHERBET

YIELD: 1 QUART

3 **ripe mangoes, peeled, seeded and quartered**	1 **cup milk**
1 **cup sugar, divided**	2 **tablespoons lime juice**
1 **envelope (¼ ounce) gelatin**	2 **egg whites**
1½ **cups boiling water**	

Assemble Fruit/Vegetable Strainer and attache to mixer. Turn to Speed 4 and strain mangoes. Measure out 1½ cups mango puree and set the rest aside.

Place ¾ cup sugar and gelatin in medium a bowl. Add boiling water and stir until completely dissolved. Cool to lukewarm. Add 1½ cups mango puree, milk, and lime juice; stir well. Freeze until partially frozen, about 1½ hours.

Place egg whites and remaining ¼ cup sugar in mixer bowl. Attach bowl and wire whip to mixer. Turn to Speed 10 and whip until stiff but not dry. Reduce to Stir Speed and quickly add mango mixture, whipping just until blended.

Freeze until firm. Let stand at room temperature a few minutes before serving.

TIP: Mangoes should be ripened at room temperature until they give slightly when pressed. When ripe, mangoes are orange-yellow in color and have a rosy blush on the side exposed to the sun.

PER SERVING: (½ CUP) ABOUT 167 CAL, 3 g PRO, 39 g CARB, 1 g FAT, 2 mg CHOL, 32 mg SOD.

Glossary
OF COOKING TERMS

AL DENTE: The literal translation of this Italian phrase is "to the tooth." It indicates a degree of doneness when cooking pasta. Al dente pasta is slightly firm and chewy, rather than soft.

BASTE: Basting is the technique of brushing, spooning, or pouring liquids over food—usually meat and poultry—as it cooks. It helps preserve moistness, adds flavor, and gives foods an attractive appearance. Melted butter, pan drippings, broth, or a combination of these ingredients are frequently used. Sometimes seasonings or flavorings are added.

BEAT: Beating is the technique of stirring or mixing vigorously. Beating introduces air into egg whites, egg yolks, and whipping cream; mixes two or more ingredients to form a homogeneous mixture; or makes a mixture smoother, lighter, and creamier. Beating can be done with a variety of tools, including a spoon, fork, wire whisk, rotary eggbeater, or electric mixer.

BLANCH: Blanching means cooking foods, most often vegetables, briefly in boiling water and then quickly cooling them in cold water. Food is blanched for one or more of the following reasons: to loosen and remove skin (tomatoes, peaches, almonds); to enhance color and reduce bitterness (raw vegetables for crudités); and to extend storage life (raw vegetables to be frozen).

BLEND: Blending is the technique of mixing together two or more ingredients until they are thoroughly combined. The ingredients may be blended together with an electric mixer or electric blender, or by hand, using a wooden spoon or wire whisk.

BOIL: To bring to a boil means to heat a liquid until bubbles break the surface. Boiling refers to cooking food in boiling water. For a "full rolling boil," bubbles break the surface continuously and cannot be stirred away.

BRAISE: Braising is a moist-heat cooking method used to tenderize tough cuts of meat or fibrous vegetables. Food is first browned in fat and then gently simmered in a small amount of liquid in a tightly covered skillet until tender. This can be done on the rangetop or in the oven. The liquid—such as water, stock, wine, or beer—often has finely chopped vegetables and herbs added for flavor.

BROIL: Broiling is the technique of cooking foods a measured distance from a direct source of heat. Both gas and electric ovens provide a means of broiling. Some rangetops have built-in grills that provide another broiling option. Grilling on a barbecue grill also fits this broad definition of broiling. The goal of broiling is to brown the exterior without overcooking the interior. Generally, the thinner the food item, the closer it should be to the heat source.

BRUSH: Brushing refers to the technique of applying a liquid such as melted butter, barbecue sauce, or glaze to the surface of food prior to or during cooking with a brush. It serves the same purpose as basting: preserving moistness, adding flavor, and giving foods an attractive appearance.

CARAMELIZE: Caramelizing is the technique of cooking sugar, sometimes with a small amount of water, to a very high temperature (between 310°F and 360°F) so that it melts into a clear brown liquid and develops a characteristic flavor. The color can vary from light golden brown to dark brown. Caramelized sugar, sometimes called "burnt sugar," is used in a variety of desserts and sauces.

CHILL: Chilling is the technique of cooling foods, usually in the refrigerator or over ice, to a temperature of 35°F to 40°F. A recipe or dish may require several hours or as long as overnight to chill thoroughly. To chill a large portion of a hot mixture such as soup or chili, separate the mixture into several small containers for quicker cooling. To chill small amounts of hot food, place the food in a bowl or saucepan over a container of crushed ice or iced water, or chill the food in the freezer for 20 to 30 minutes.

CHOP: Chopping is the technique of cutting food into small, irregularly shaped pieces. Although the term does not designate a specific size, most cooks would suggest that food be chopped into approximately ¼-inch pieces. Chopped food is larger than minced food and more irregularly cut than diced food. Recipe directions may call for a coarsely chopped or a finely chopped ingredient.

COAT: To coat means to cover food with an outer layer, usually fine or powdery, using ingredients such as flour, crumbs, cornmeal, or sugar. With foods such as chicken, fish fillets, and eggplant, this coating is preliminary to frying or baking and provides a crispy exterior. Such foods are often first rolled in eggs or milk so the coating adheres. Some cookies are coated with sugar before or after baking.

COMBINE: Combining is the process of mixing two or more liquid or dry ingredients together to make them a uniform mixture.

CORE: Coring means to remove the center seed-bearing structure of a fruit or vegetable. The most commonly cored foods are apples, pears, pineapple, zucchini, and cucumbers. First cutting the food into quarters and then cutting out the center core can accomplish coring with a small knife. A utensil specially designed to remove the core of specific whole fruits and vegetables is known as a corer. The most common corers are for apples, pears, and pineapple.

CRUMBLE: To crumble means to break food into small pieces of irregular size. It is usually done with the fingers. Ingredients often crumbled include blue cheese and bacon. Both foods can be purchased in the supermarket already crumbled.

CRUSH: Crushing means reducing a food, such as crackers, to small fine particles by rolling with a rolling pin or pounding with a mortar and pestle. A food processor or blender also works well. Fruit can be crushed to extract its juices. Garlic is sometimes crushed with the flat side of a knife blade or garlic press to release its flavor.

CUTTING IN: Cutting in is the technique used to combine a chilled solid fat such as shortening or butter with dry ingredients such as flour so that the resulting mixture is in coarse, small pieces. A fork, two table knives, fingers, or a pastry blender may be used. If using a food processor, be careful not to over-mix the ingredients. This process is used to make biscuits, scones, pie pastry, and some cookies.

DEGLAZE: Deglazing is the technique used to retrieve the flavorful bits that adhere to a pan after a food, usually meat, has been browned and the excess fat has been drained. While the pan is still hot, a small amount of liquid (water, wine, or broth) is added and stirred to loosen the browned bits in the pan. The resulting liquid is used as a base for sauces and gravies.

DEGREASE: Degreasing is a technique used to remove fat from the surface of a liquid such as soup or stock. It can be accomplished in several ways. First remove the soup or stock from the heat and allow it to stand briefly until the fat rises. The quickest degreasing method is to skim off the fat using a large spoon. If the fat to be removed is animal fat, the liquid may be chilled; the animal fat will harden, making it easy to lift off.

DICE: To dice is to cut food into small cubes that are uniform in size. The smallest dice, which is about $\frac{1}{8}$ of an inch, is best suited for delicate garnishing. More typical are sizes between $\frac{1}{4}$ and $\frac{1}{2}$ of an inch. Dicing is distinguished from chopping and mincing by the care taken to achieve a uniform size for an attractive presentation.

DOT: This term, generally used in cooking as "to dot with butter," refers to cutting butter (or margarine) into small bits and scattering them over a food. This technique allows the butter to melt evenly. It also keeps the food moist, adds richness, and can promote browning.

DUST: Dusting is a technique used to lightly coat a food, before or after cooking, with a powdery ingredient such as flour or powdered sugar. The ingredient may be sprinkled on using your fingers or shaken from a small sieve or a container with holes on the top. A greased baking pan can be dusted with flour before it is filled, a technique also known as "flouring."

FLAKE: To flake refers to the technique of separating or breaking off small pieces or layers of a food using a utensil, such as a fork. For example, cooked fish fillets may be flaked for use in a salad or main dish.

FLOUR: To flour means to apply a light coating of flour to a food or piece of equipment. Applied to food, the flour dries the surface. This helps food brown better when frying or sautéing, and keeps food such as raisins from sticking together. Baking pans are floured for better release characteristics and to produce thin, crisp crusts. Rolling pins, biscuit cutters, cookie cutters, and work surfaces are floured to prevent doughs from sticking to them.

FOLD: Folding is a specialized technique for combining two ingredients or mixtures, one of which usually has been aerated, such as whipped cream or egg whites. It is best done by placing the airy mixture on top of the other and, with a rubber spatula, gently but quickly cutting through to the bottom and turning the ingredients over with a rolling motion. The bowl is rotated a quarter-turn each time and the process repeated until the mixtures are combined with as little loss in volume as possible. Care must be taken not to stir, beat, or overmix. Fruit pieces, chips, or nuts may be folded into an airy mixture using the same technique.

FRY: Frying refers to the technique of cooking foods in hot fat, usually vegetable oil. Proper fat temperature is critical to a successful result. The ideal temperature produces a crisp exterior and a moist, perfectly cooked interior; too high a temperature will burn the food, and too low a temperature will result in food absorbing excessive fat. A deep-fat thermometer is essential to determining the temperature of the fat. Deep-fried foods are submerged or floated in hot fat in a large heavy saucepan or Dutch oven. Electric deep fryers fitted with wire baskets are available. Pan-frying refers to cooking food in a skillet in a small amount of fat that does not cover the food.

GRATE: Grating refers to the technique of making very small particles from a firm food like carrots, lemon peel, or Parmesan cheese by rubbing it along a coarse surface with small, sharp protrusions, usually a metal kitchen grater. Food may also be grated in a food processor using a specialized metal blade.

KNEAD: Kneading refers to the technique of manipulating bread dough in order to develop the protein in flour, called gluten, to ensure the structure of the finished product. Kneading also aids in combining the dough ingredients. Biscuit dough is lightly kneaded—only about 10 times—whereas yeast doughs may be vigorously kneaded for several minutes.

MASH: To mash is to crush a food into a soft, smooth mixture, as in mashed potatoes or bananas. It can be done with a tool called a potato masher or with an electric mixer. Small amounts of food, such as one or two bananas or a few hard-cooked egg yolks, can be mashed with a fork. For best results, make sure that potatoes are fully cooked so they are soft enough to become completely smooth.

MINCE: Mincing refers to the technique of chopping food into very tiny, irregular pieces. Minced food is smaller than chopped food. Flavorful seasonings, such as garlic and fresh herbs, are often minced to distribute their flavor more evenly throughout a dish.

PURÉE: To purée means to mash or strain a soft or cooked food until it has a smooth consistency. This can be done with a food processor, sieve, blender, or food mill. For best results, the food must be naturally soft, such as raspberries or ripe pears, or cooked until it is completely tender. Puréed foods are used as sauces and as ingredients in other sweet or savory dishes. The term also refers to the foods that result from the process.

REDUCE: To reduce is to boil a liquid, usually a sauce, until its volume has been decreased through evaporation. This results in a more intense flavor and thicker consistency. Typically, $1/3$ or $1/2$ of their original volume reduces sauces. Use a pan with a wide bottom to shorten preparation time. The reduced product is referred to as a "reduction." Since the flavor of the seasonings will also become concentrated when a sauce is reduced, add the seasonings to the sauce after it has been reduced.

ROAST: Roasting involves cooking poultry and large tender cuts of meat in the oven in an uncovered pan. Roasting produces a nicely browned exterior and a moist interior. Roasting vegetables intensifies their natural sweetness. Vegetables such as onions and carrots can be roasted alongside meat. Many vegetables can be roasted and served as a side dish or used as ingredients in other dishes.

ROLL OUT: To roll out means to flatten dough into an even layer using a rolling pin. To roll out pastry or cookie dough, place the dough—which should be in the shape of a disc—on a floured surface, such as a counter, pastry cloth, or a large cutting board. Lightly flour your hands and the rolling pin. Place the rolling pin across the center of the dough. With several light strokes, roll the rolling pin away from you toward the edge of the dough. Turn the dough a quarter-turn and roll again from the center to the edge. Repeat this process until the dough is the desired thickness. If the dough becomes sticky, dust it and the rolling pin with flour. If the dough sticks to the surface, gently fold back the edge of the dough and dust the surface underneath the dough with flour.

SAUTÉ: Sautéing is the technique of rapidly cooking or browning food in a small amount of fat in a skillet or sauté pan. The food is constantly stirred, turned, or tossed to keep it from sticking or burning. Thin, tender cuts of meat—such as steaks, lamb chops, sliced pork tenderloin, flattened chicken breasts, and fish fillets—are candidates for sautéing. The objective is to brown the food on the outside in the time needed to cook the interior. This requires medium-high heat. Oil can withstand the higher heat needed for sautéing. For flavor, a little butter can be added to the oil, but do not use only butter or margarine because it will burn before the food browns.

SIFT: Sifting is the technique of passing a dry ingredient such as flour or powdered sugar through the fine mesh of a sieve or sifter for the purpose of breaking up lumps and making it lighter in texture. Sifting results in finer baked goods and smoother frostings. Most all-purpose flour is pre-sifted, eliminating the need for sifting. Cake flour is generally sifted before using. Spoon the ingredient into the sieve and push it through the mesh screen using a metal spoon or rubber spatula.

SIMMER: To simmer is to cook a liquid or a food in a liquid with gentle heat just below the boiling point. Small bubbles slowly rising to the surface of the liquid indicate simmering.

SLIVER: To sliver is the technique of cutting food into thin strips or pieces. Basil and garlic are two ingredients that may be identified as slivered in a recipe. The word "sliver" may also refer to a long, thin strip of food or a small wedge of a pie.

STEAM: Steaming is a method of cooking food, usually vegetables, in the steam given off by boiling water. The food is held above, but not in, the boiling or simmering water in a covered pan. The steam swirls around the food and cooks it with an intense, moist heat. Steaming helps to retain flavor, color, shape, texture, and many of the vitamins and minerals. Steaming is often done in a two-pan steamer, a steamer basket, or a bamboo steamer.

STRAIN: Straining refers to the technique of pouring a liquid through the small holes of a strainer or the wires mesh of a sieve to remove lumps or unwanted particles.

TOAST: Toasting is the technique of browning foods by means of dry heat. Bread products, nuts, seeds, and coconut are commonly toasted. Toasting is done in a toaster, toaster oven, oven, or skillet, or under the broiler. The purpose of toasting bread is to brown, crisp, and dry it. Nuts, seeds, and coconut are toasted to intensify their flavor.

WHIP: To whip refers to the technique of beating ingredients such as egg whites and whipping cream with a wire whisk or electric mixer in order to incorporate air and increase their volume. This results in a light, fluffy texture.

WHISK: Whisking is the technique of stirring, beating, or whipping foods with a wire whisk. If you do not have a whisk, you can use a wooden spoon if the purpose is to blend ingredients. For whipping foods, an electric mixer can be used instead.

Almond Dacquoise........................140

Almond Poppy Seed Cookies........116

Appetizer Cream Puffs....................10

APPETIZERS

Appetizer Cream Puffs 10

Broccoli-Cheese Bake.................27

Crabmeat Dip 28

Fiesta Cheesecake Appetizer......16

French Onion Soup....................22

Herbed Whipped Squash...........24

Hummus 28

Mashed Potatoes 30

Meatball Hors D'Oeuvres...........18

Mushroom-Onion Tartlets 20

Nutty Cheese Ball 16

Potato Pancakes 31

Roquefort Nut Spread 22

Spinach and Cheese Crostini......29

Sweet Potato Puff 12

Swiss Bacon Canapés................24

Tiropetas...................................14

Apple Crumb Coffee Cake.............53

Applesauce Cake...........................81

Baking Powder Biscuits 38

BAR COOKIES

Blondies...................................108

Double-Decker Butterscotch
  Brownies 114

Fudge Brownies........................118

Lemon Cream Cheese Bars.......126

Basic Egg Noodle Pasta 72

Black Bean Frittata 60

Blondies.....................................108

Blueberry Macadamia Nut Swirl
  Coffee Cake................................86

Bolognese Sauce 62

Bourbon Street Beignets 46

Braised Lamb Mediterranean 58

Brioche Ring 55

Broccoli-Cheese Bake 27

Brown Edge Wafers 106

Buttercream Frosting 90

CAKES

Apple Crumb Coffee Cake 53

Applesauce Cake 81

Blueberry Macadamia Nut
  Swirl Coffee Cake 86

Cappuccino Fudge Cupcakes 80

Caramel Walnut Banana Torte 84

Carrot Cake..............................98

Chocolate Roll 92

Easy White Cake.....................100

Old-Fashioned Pound Cake 88

Quick Yellow Cake 90

Sour Cream Bundt Cake...........101

Sunshine Chiffon Cake..............99

CANDIES

Chocolate Fudge 105

Creamy No-Cook Mints 104

Divinity 122

Cappuccino Fudge Cupcakes 80

Caramel Crème Frosting.................94

Caramel Walnut Banana Torte 84

Carrot Cake 98

Cheese Braid..............................54

Cheese-Stuffed Shells......................64

Chicken and Mushroom Casserole
with Cheese Puff Topping..............66

Chinese Noodles 68

CHOCOLATE

Almond Dacquoise 140

Cappuccino Fudge Cupcakes 80

Chocolate Frosting 96

Chocolate Fudge 105

Chocolate Pecan Pie 130

Chocolate Roll 92

Double Chocolate Mousse
with Raspberry Sauce 150

Double-Decker Butterscotch
Brownies 114

Fudge Brownies.......................118

Pots de Crème au Chocolat 146

Wafer Torte..............................138

Chocolate Chip Cookies...............120

Chocolate Frosting 96

Chocolate Fudge 105

Chocolate Pecan Pie 130

Chocolate Roll 92

COOKIES

Almond Poppy Seed
Cookies................................116

Brown Edge Wafers.................106

Chocolate Chip Cookies 120

Macadamia Chocolate
Chunk Cookies....................110

Macaroons 106

Peanut Butter Cookies 124

Pecan Shortbread Cookies 112

Raisin-Apricot Oatmeal
Cookies................................127

Country Pear Pie 130

Crabmeat Dip..............................28

Creamy No-Cook Mints...............104

DIPS AND SPREADS

Crabmeat Dip 28

Fiesta Cheesecake Appetizer 16

Hummus 28

Nutty Cheese Ball 16

Roquefort Nut Spread 22

Divinity 122

Double Chocolate Mousse
With Raspberry Sauce 150

Double-Decker Butterscotch
Brownies...................................114

Easy White Cake........................100

ENTREÉS

Black Bean Frittata 60

Braised Lamb Mediterranean 58

Cheese-Stuffed Shells 64

Chicken and Mushroom
Casserole with Cheese
Puff Topping..........................66

Chinese Noodles.......................68

Mushroom Swiss Onion
Quiche..................................75

Osso Buco 59

Pork Chops with Sweet
    Potatoes and Apples...............77
Shrimp Gumbo..........................76
Spinach Pasta Pomodoro...........70

Fiesta Cheesecake Appetizer 16
Fluffy Frosting 82
French Onion Soup 22

FROSTINGS
Buttercream Frosting...................90
Caramel Crème Frosting.............94
Chocolate Frosting 96
Fluffy Frosting 82
Orange Cream Cheese
    Frosting 100
Fudge Brownies 118

Garlic Pull-Apart Bread 44
German Apple Pancakes 52

Herbed Whipped Squash 24
Hidden Pumpkin Pie 144
Horseradish Sauce 68
Hummus..28

Key Lime Pie 132

Lemon Cream Cheese Bars 126
Lemon Curd Tart with Fresh
    Blueberries 142
Lemon Soufflé 148
Lemon Tea Bread 40
Lemony Light Cheesecake 149

Macadamia Chocolate Chunk
    Cookies 110
Macaroons....................................106

Mango Sherbet..........................151
Mashed Potatoes 30
Mayonnaise 26
Meatball Hors D'Oeuvres 18
Mushroom Swiss Onion Quiche 75
Mushroom-Onion Tartlets 20

Nutty Cheese Ball 16

Old-Fashioned Pound Cake............88
Orange Cream Cheese Frosting 100
Orange Muffins 36
Osso Buco....................................59

Panettone 48

PASTAS
Basic Egg Noodle Pasta 72
Cheese-Stuffed Shells 64
Spinach Pasta 70
Whole Wheat Pasta 74

PASTA SAUCES
Bolognese Sauce 62
Chinese Noodles 68
Pesto Sauce...............................74
Spinach Pasta Pomodoro...........70

Peanut Butter Cookies 124
Pecan Shortbread Cookies............112
Pesto Sauce 74

PIES
Chocolate Pecan Pie 130
Country Pear Pie.......................130
Hidden Pumpkin Pie.................144

Key Lime Pie...........................132

Lemon Curd Tart with Fresh
    Blueberries......................142

Pie Pastry...............................131

Rustic Apple Tart....................134

Vanilla Cream Pie...................136

Pie Pastry 131

Pita Bread 35

Popovers 34

Poppy Seed Dressing 31

Pork Chops with Sweet Potatoes
  and Apples 77

Potato Pancakes............................31

Pots de Crème Au Chocolat 146

QUICK BREADS

Baking Powder Biscuits...............38

German Apple Pancakes............52

Lemon Tea Bread 40

Orange Muffins 36

Popovers...................................34

Raisin-Wheat Muffins 34

Scones......................................42

Sour Cream Soda Bread 52

Quick Yellow Cake............................90

Raisin-Apricot Oatmeal Cookies 127

Raisin-Wheat Muffins.......................34

Rouquefort Nut Spread....................22

Russian Black Bread 50

Rustic Apple Tart 134

SALAD DRESSINGS

Mayonnaise...............................26

Poppy Seed Dressing 31

Scones...42

Shrimp Gumbo 76

Sour Cream Bundt Cake 101

Sour Cream Soda Bread..................52

Spinach and Cheese Crostini 29

Spinach Pasta.................................70

Spinach Pasta Pomodoro 70

Sunshine Chiffon Cake 99

Sweet Potato Puff 12

Swiss Bacon Canapés 24

Tiropetas 14

Vanilla Cream Pie 136

VEGETABLE SIDES

Broccoli-Cheese Bake.................27

Herbed Whipped Squash...........24

Mashed Potatoes 30

Potato Pancakes 31

Sweet Potato Puff 12

Wafer Torte 138

Whole Wheat Pasta.......................74

YEAST BREADS

Apple Crumb Coffee Cake 53

Bourbon Street Beignets..............46

Brioche Ring..............................55

Cheese Braid 54

Garlic Pull-Apart Bread..............44

Panettone..................................48

Pita Bread 35

Russian Black Bread...................50